Global Custody

Global Custody

The Industry, the Strategies and the Competitive Opportunities

JAMES ESSINGER

FINANCIAL TIMES

PRENTICE HALL

Pearson Education Limited

Head Office:
Edinburgh Gate
Harlow CM20 2JE
Tel: +44 (0) 1279 623623
Fax: +44 (0) 1279 431059

London Office:
128 Long Acre, London WC2E 9AN
Tel: +44 (0)171 447 2000
Fax: +44 (0)171 240 5771

———————————

First published in Great Britain in 1999

ISBN 0 273 64441 6

British Library Cataloguing in Publication Data
A CIP catalogue record for this book can be obtained
from the British Library.

1 3 5 7 9 10 8 6 4 2

Typeset by
Northern Phototypesetting Co. Ltd, Bolton.
Printed and bound in Great Britain by
Biddles Ltd, Guildford & King's Lynn.

*The Publishers' policy is to use paper manufactured
from sustainable forests.*

About the Author

James Essinger holds an MA in English Language and Literature from Lincoln College, Oxford. He writes on financial technology for a wide range of publications in the US and UK, and has been a frequent contributor to *Global Custodian*, the leading journal of the global custody industry, as well as custody correspondent for the UK journal *Investment and Pensions Europe*. James has published numerous other books and reports on banking technology, the financial sector and business management, including *The FT Handbook of Investment Management*. He also writes popular science and fiction.

CONTENTS

ACKNOWLEDGEMENTS

I gratefully acknowledge the kind assistance of the following people and organisations in preparing this book:

David Bailey (Bank of Bermuda), Laurie Baker (Lloyds Bank Securities Services), Dave Batten (RBS Trust), Penny Biggs (Northern Trust), Emma Crabtree (Morgan Stanley), Roger Fishwick (Prudential Portfolio Managers), Debbie Freshwater (Midland Securities Services), Peter Gnepf (International Securities Services Association), Chris Hibben (IMRO), Curt Kohlberg (Kohlberg & Associates), Laura Hoult (Brown Brothers Harriman), Avis Judd (Chase Manhattan), Gordon Lindsay (RBS Trust), Simon Murray (Thomas Murray), David Newman (Morgan Stanley), Ron Porter (Lloyds Bank Securities Services), Chris Rees (Charteris), Duncan Reid (Zergo), Tony Solway (Henderson Investment Services), Pierre Slechten (Euroclear), Mark Tennant (Chase Manhattan), Dick Vesey (Lloyds Bank Securities Services), David Watson (Lloyds Bank Securities Services).

I would like to thank Helen Wylie for her assistance, and the Institute for International Research Limited for allowing me to attend, as an observer, its Ninth International Global Custody Forum in London on 29 and 30 October, 1998.

My sincere thanks are also due to Linda Dhondy and Martha Fausset for their careful help with the production of this book, and to Richard Stagg, my publisher at Financial Times Prentice Hall.

INTRODUCTION   1

The term 'global custody' describes both a major international industry and a set of services relating to the administration of investments made *outside* the country where the investor is located.

Since the start of the 1980s, when due to changes in the policy of several governments – especially those in the US and UK – large-scale overseas investment became not only permitted but actively encouraged, the volume of assets held by banks practising global custody has dramatically increased. It would nowadays be no exaggeration to describe the global custody industry as a major constituent element of the world's financial industry.

Organizations which provide global custody services do not invest funds themselves (although they may do so via a completely separate department) but they *hold* assets on behalf of their clients in special accounts which are designated nominee accounts, meaning that they exist for the benefit of whichever person or organization is named as the beneficiary.

What is the precise scale of the international global custody industry? This is a matter for some debate and requires extremely meticulous research. The fundamental challenge here is that organizations which practice global custody use different ways of counting the assets which they hold on behalf of their investor clients.

There are two basic types of assets in this respect: those which the organization holds in the country where it operates and those which the organization holds abroad, either via its foreign offices or via other agent banks with which it works. Global custody, strictly speaking, relates to those assets held abroad. Unfortunately, not every organization which practises global custody differentiates between these two types of assets. However, I believe that the figure of $24 trillion (i.e. $24,000,000,000,000) quoted by the journal *Global Custodian* as the level which total global funds in custody were likely to reach during 1998, is accurate. Similarly, according to *Global Custodian*, about 30 per cent of this total relates to assets which are held by global custody organizations outside the country where the organization is based: whether the assets are held on behalf of foreign or domestic clients. This suggests that the total sum of assets held strictly in global custody is about $7.2 trillion. Incidentally, the magazine also estimates that, globally, about 25 per cent of all stock trades made today are cross-border. If these custodial positions produced an average yield or dividend payment of, say, 5 per cent, the total yield would be about $300 billion, which I would tentatively suggest as a total for the yield of those assets held under global custody, worldwide.

True, the figure of $24 trillion does not accommodate assets held by a global custody practitioner in the case where the assets are held in the country where the practitioner is located but owned by an investor abroad. However, this does not compromise the figures as much as might be expected, since the vast majority of assets held abroad are held by a bank that is the same nationality as the investor.

One particularly important fact about the global custody business is the enormous domination of the US as a location of invested assets, whether the assets originate from US or non-US investors. For example, the most up-to-date figures released by the New York-based research organization Buttonwood International suggest that about 70 per cent of the world's investment made in securities are held in the US. The next most important country in this respect is the UK, which has a comparatively modest 6.9%, and then followed by France, with 2.5%. Japan is a relatively small player in terms of being a location for investors' assets, with only about 1 per cent of total invested assets. Incidentally, Buttonwood International has an aggregate figure for assets held in custody of well in excess of $14 trillion, which seems a useful corroboration of the *Global Custodian* figures.

Global custody plays an essential role in achieving and/or facilitating all of the following:

- the security of cross-border investments;
- the collection and forwarding to investors of revenue from cross-border investments;
- the control which investors have over their cross-border investments, especially in terms of their knowledge of corporate actions taken by the organizations in whose securities they invest;
- investor confidence in the usefulness and profitability of cross-border investments;
- the international flow of investment capital.

It follows from this that, even though the global custody industry is hardly known outside the financial world, and even though many who work within the financial sector are largely or completely unaware of its existence, the industry plays an absolutely essential role in enabling the creation of national wealth based upon funding by investments coming from abroad. It is no exaggeration to say that without the global custody business, the world would be a much poorer place.

From the service perspective, we can define 'global custody' as *a range of services relating to the administration of cross-border investments*.

As we have already seen, it is necessary to draw a clear distinction between those services which relate to *domestic* investments – that is, investments which are made and held in the country where the investor is located – and *cross-border* investments – that is, where the investment is made and held outside the country where the investor is located.

For reasons of simplicity, the term global custody is often abbreviated in this book, as in the industry itself, to 'custody'.

Why have I decided to make the focus of this book global custody rather than domestic custody? The reasons are as follows.

● The legal, tax-related and general administrative complexities of cross-border investment mean that global custody presents a particular and significant challenge to investors: that is, they frequently need assistance with administrative services relating to their cross-border investments and are less likely to be able to handle these administrative requirements themselves. Note that what is true of cross-border investments generally is particularly true of investments in emerging markets, where local market conditions are often extremely difficult and where only a local bank has any chance at all of dealing with them. To take just two examples, in Russia the securities system is still based around paper-held registration, and because there are so many accidental errors and erasures there is the constant danger that names of stockholders will be deleted. This danger applies particularly to foreign investors, who need local representation in order to ensure that they are continuously registered as owners of the securities in question. Another example is Hungary, where settlement of securities transactions is extremely informal and not very systematic. One of my research sources described it as 'two fellows in a café'. Clearly, any investor wishing to invest securely in such a market will need competent, energetic and vigilant local representation.

● Closely related to the above point is the fact that most investors tend to regard their cross-border investments as carrying more prospects for higher return (with, as one might expect, the downside of higher risk) than their domestic investments. There are two rationales for this. First, cross-border investments are likely to be less well-known to other investors than are domestic investments, with the result that there may be a better chance of achieving exceptional return. Second, most fund managers today practise some kind of diversification strategy (which accords with the principles of modern portfolio theory) and as fund managers are frequently substantially invested in major domestic stocks, the only route available for diversification is in foreign securities. In the extremely competitive climate in which all investors – and particularly specialized investment management organizations who manage investments on behalf of highly demanding clients – find themselves, maximizing the performance of cross-border investments is a crucial element in maximizing overall competitiveness. Global custody has a key role to play in this, by ensuring that local administrative processes are properly handled and that information regarding investments (and local market conditions) is rapidly relayed to investors. Organizations offering global custody services *actually reduce the risk of cross-border investments*. This is the crucial point: the reduction of risk.

● At a purely financial level, proper use of global custody services can increase the revenue from an investment holding and thereby assist greatly with the performance of a fund. This is an important point not only for investors themselves, who will end up with more money, but also for those specialized organizations whose business is to manage investments on behalf of a variety of types of funds, and whose commercial success therefore depends considerably on how successful they are at enhancing performance.

● All global custodians offer domestic custody services. For many investors, therefore, selecting the right custodian at a global level will automatically solve the problem of selecting a domestic custodian. Because selecting a global custodian is a more complex process, it makes sense to focus on this. Note, however, that some investors do have a policy of using a different custodian for their domestic and global custody requirements.

It is essential to emphasize that global custody plays an absolutely fundamental role in the success of any fund managers, institutional investor or any other organisation which is investing funds. Fortunately, for sales of this book, the essential nature of this role is increasingly recognized by fund managers and institutional investors around the world.

The reason why global custody is so important relates to the nature of the investment management business today. Anybody who delves into this business in any detail quickly realizes that, while the ability of individual talented fund managers to achieve better-than-average fund performance can never be ruled out, in general the Efficient Markets Hypothesis (EMH) – which holds that when markets are efficient (as most modern securities markets are regarded as being), the prices of securities traded on those markets will reflect all available information – represents a pretty solid argument against any one fund manager being able to obtain *consistently* better-than-average performance.

If the EMH is valid, and the general consensus within the fund management business today is that it is, the great efficiency of modern information technology in spreading information about securities across all market participants and interested persons in a very short space of time, means that the opportunities for one person or organization to obtain legal (i.e. not inside) information about a security or group of securities are few and far between.

This being the case, modern portfolio theory suggests that the only way to give oneself a realistic chance of winning consistent better-than-average investment results is to take on excessive amounts of risk. Taking on these excessive levels of risk is precisely what the vast majority of institutional investors do not want to do.

It follows, therefore, that none of us should be surprised if, on average, most active fund managers (as opposed to passive managers who use indexation techniques, the increasing popularity of which is further corroboration of the validity of the EMH) tend to obtain performance results which are roughly similar to one another's.

In this atmosphere, sheer common sense suggests that any method which institutional investors can use to maximize their fund performance and overall levels of customer service without taking on undue risk in their securities positions must be useful – if not essential – improvements in business practice. Even making the cultural decision throughout the organisation to take every step to give clients careful and thoughtful attention can only be a good decision. Yet there is one area where, frequently, a great deal of competitive advantage can be obtained without client funds being put at risk at all. This is the area of global custody.

Global custody, as I have already explained, covers a wide range of administrative services relating to the actual holding of securities. As one might expect, there is a clear connection between the effectiveness and efficiency with which these services are carried out and the overall efficiency of the service which the institutional investor is offering to its customers. However, it would be a mistake to imagine that these services are only purely administrative ones. In many cases they relate to the very core of the process of looking after client funds and assets, and can directly generate revenue for the client. Properly managed, good global custody can give investment managers the prospect of higher return on a fund, and thereby higher performance, without the need to take on higher levels of risk.

This explains why, today, everybody in the investment management industry is talking about global custody. This explains why global custody is one of the fastest-growing industries in the wholesale banking sector.

This book is primarily designed for investors. It will, however, also be of use to traders, custodians, consultants and strategists as well as system designers and integrators with a particular involvement in the global custody industry. The book is designed to be a hands-on publication with maximum practical utility for the demands of readers operating in the highly competitive international securities industry. It is a book for the desk-top, not the bookshelf. My aim is to provide readers with state-of-the-art information and guidance directed at helping them make the most of global custody insofar as the industry intersects with their own professional needs, and consequently to make both them, and their organizations, more successful.

GLOBAL CUSTODY AND INVESTORS

2

MORE DEFINITIONS

We have already seen how 'global custody' differs from 'domestic custody' and that because the global custody function is the more complex and demanding of the two, it makes sense to focus the analysis contained in this book on the global function. One might go even further, and say that, in a sense, domestic custody is a subset of global custody, because every service carried out at a domestic level by a domestic custodian must also be carried out by a global custodian, but at a global level.

Let's take some more definitions on board.

A 'global custodian' is any organization which provides global custody services as the principal, or the only, part of its business. Note that in this book, for simplicity, the term global custodian is often abbreviated to 'custodian'.

Global custodians are usually large commercial banks, many of which have offices around the world. When they are working for an investor client in a number of national locations, they will generally either make use of their own proprietary foreign offices, or else use another, third-party, bank with which they have a special relationship. Frequently this special relationship will be the result of a rigorous selection process.

Some global custodians are investment banks. However, in

recent years there has been a definite tendency for investment banks to pull out of offering the global custody function. In fact, global custody does not really sit very comfortably within the investment banking function. Investment banking is ultimately the highly 'entrepreneurial' end of banking: investment bankers 'work' their banks' capital hard in order to make money for their bank and earn bonuses. Global custody, on the other hand, while certainly incorporating some services which have the potential to win investors a considerable degree of competitive edge, is principally a record-keeping, account-maintaining service: one that is more in harmony with the traditions of retail and wholesale banking than investment banking.

Some investors attempt to undertake their own global custody. This practice is expressly forbidden or restricted by some national regulatory frameworks (for example, US pension funds are not allowed to act as their own custodians), but even where it is permitted there is an increasing consensus that this is not how things should be done. By definition, an organization that is good at investment management is an investment specialist, and an investment specialist will not also be a custody specialist. There seems little need to say any more about the matter than that. We live in an age when levels of competitiveness between different organizations are so intense that specialization of function is usually essential simply to survive, let alone to flourish. Investors should perhaps stick to what they do best, and let global custodians do the same.

Another term needing definition is the notion of the 'agent bank' or 'sub-custodian'. These are *banks hired by a global custodian (which is often known as the 'lead custodian') on a contractual basis in order to undertake domestic custody activity in a country or region where the global custody does not have a presence at all, or has insufficient expertise.* The role of the sub-custodian is, as one might imagine, extremely important as offering one custodian the chance to gain a competitive edge, because expertise in specific countries' settlement and securities administration requirements is one area where one global custody can establish a lead over another. This is particularly the case as far as emerging markets are concerned.

Note, incidentally, that just because a bank is an agent bank rather than a global custodian, does not mean that its service is inherently any less good. Many highly successful agent banks have carved out niches in their domestic markets which are the envy of any organization involved in custody. Ultimately, just as it is said that politics is essentially always local, a strong case could be made that custody, too, is always local, even though the ultimate caretaker may be a large international bank which is operating as a global custodian. What really matters is not the way in which a bank describes itself but rather the efficiency and attention to detail of its services. That said, the distinction between banks offering an international, truly *global* service and those whose business remit is essentially domestic is an important one and needs to be borne in mind.

I use the term 'investor' in this book to refer to *any person or (more often) organization which is making investments abroad and may therefore wish to make use of the services of a global custodian.* The investors discussed in this book are usually institutional investors. I sometimes use this term in full, but more often use the term investor to avoid tedious repetitions. Private investors will usually not use the service of a global custodian directly, although they may do if they have substantial foreign holdings. Note that in some contexts in this book I also use the term 'client' to denote the investor.

This book primarily caters for the following investors.

● **Institutional investors**. These are large organizations whose reason for being in business is to act as a channel for funds contributed by a large number of people in the form of regular or single premiums, regular or single investments or other types of payment such as donations. The basic rationale for the existence of institutional investors is that where a large number of investors pool their resources, they can benefit from economies of scale – and commission/transaction costs which can be spread over all participants – from which they could not benefit if they were investing relatively small amounts singly. Another important rationale is simply that the people involved will very likely not want to be participants in an investment process in any active sense because they have their own jobs to do. In other words, they delegate their investment activity to a large professional organization which specializes in this area. Examples of institutional investors are pension funds, life assurance companies, insurance companies and charities. Many local authorities and government bodies also act in effect as institutional investors because they invest money obtained from the public, but they carry out other activities as well, and cannot strictly speaking be described as institutional investors in the proper sense of the word. Note that many institutional investors are household names. For example, the Prudential, Legal & General, Scottish Widows, Abbey Life and Oxfam are all institutional investors of one kind or another.

- **Private investors** with large foreign holdings of stock and other investment instruments.
- **Investment management organizations** whose business it is to manage assets on behalf of a diverse range of clients. Strictly speaking, these organizations are themselves institutional investors, but because they tend to manage money only on behalf of large corporations or other formal investment vehicles, rather than on behalf of private individuals entirely, they need slightly different treatment here. Many such organizations do manage investments for private investors, but only for those with substantial funds to invest.

Specialized investment management organisations play an extremely important role in the global custody industry because of their considerable financial muscle. They frequently find themselves having the opportunity to recommend to their own clients which custodians should be used, although it is true that some clients will have their own views on this and will not want to be advised on the matter.

Which types of organizations make use of the services of specialized investment management firms? The vast majority of such firms' clients are pension funds. But why do some pension funds prefer to use the services of such firms rather than act as principals in the investment process? Simply because some pension funds are not big enough to derive significant economies of scale from their investment activity.

Furthermore, acting as a principal in the investment process is often surprisingly expensive. For one thing, it is necessary at the very least to employ one full-time investment manager, and then to equip him or her with office space and access to information from around the world about the prices and availability of securities. Developing an in-house investment facility is unlikely to cost less than £100,000 annually and may cost a great deal more. Not surprisingly, many smaller pension funds regard this as highly uneconomical and consequently prefer to use the services of a specialized fund manager.

THE ORIGINS OF THE GLOBAL CUSTODY INDUSTRY

Many of the services provided by global custodians have been supplied by banks to investors since the nineteenth century. The major Scottish banks, in particular, can date their experience of looking after the administrative and income collection requirements of overseas investors back to the days when capital accumulated by

Scotland's prudent savers helped to build the railroads and cities of North America.

It is salutary to remember – when technology and global marketing concepts play such a key role in the provision and reception of global custody services – that in many respects the spiritual home of global custody is not in the digitized communication industry, but in the austere but noble buildings of Edinburgh's financial centre.

Historically, the global custody function would have been regarded, in effect, as part of the service which banks offered to those of their customers who held overseas investments. These services would involve the bank ensuring that once the investment opportunity had been assessed by the bank as bona fide, and the general prospects for returns assessed and found viable, the investment capital was channelled to the respective overseas recipient with the minimum of delay. The bank would also provide a secure vault for the storage of share certificates, debentures and other valuable documents.

The overseas branch of the bank (or a trusted bank which was being used as an agent bank) would relay dividend payments, bonuses and other payments to investors as rapidly as contemporary technology allowed. The range of service provided was generally limited to safe custody and income collection, with some settlement activity and processing and relaying of details of corporate actions.

It was not until the mid-1970s that the concept of global custody as an industry in its own right began to develop. The usual credit for devising the term global custody and using it as the basis for marketing a range of related services, is given to the Chase Manhattan Bank, which was employing the term 'global custody' in its corporate literature as early as 1974. Chase Manhattan is still one of the world's leading global custodians.

It is no coincidence that the term global custody was first

recorded in 1974, because it was in that year, in the US, that the Employment Retirement Income Security Act (ERISA) became law. The Act, which was passed as a measure to protect pension funds, stipulated that US pension funds could not act as custodians of their own funds. In effect, the Act created a requirement for pension funds to hold their funds at a separate bank. The ERISA also stipulated that only US banks could carry out the custodian function for US pension funds.

One obvious consequence of the ERISA was increased demand, at a purely domestic level, for the service of US banks which could handle the custody, accounting, and associated requirements of pension funds. There was also a knock-on effect, with many other institutional investors feeling that their own holdings also ought to be held and administered by separate custodians.

Although the overall effect of the Act was, predictably enough, to foster an increase in domestic custody, it also led to a great increase in demand for a banking service which could handle the custody and related requirements of the overseas holdings of US investors. This resulted in US custodians seeking to establish a greater presence overseas. The provision and promotion of global custody service became an important part of their marketing strategy.

Today, the ERISA legislation means that, at least in the US, custody and investment are legally separate activities. This particular provision is covered by clause number 17f5 in the ERISA: an important clause which is frequently referred to by its number within the global custody industry; with the expectation that everyone will know what this means.

FORCES WHICH GOVERN THE DEVELOPMENT OF THE GLOBAL CUSTODY INDUSTRY

The ERISA is an important example of how national legislation can act as a force which drives the global custody industry forward. However, legislation is only one such force.

It is reasonable to identify four principal driving factors which govern the pace of development of the global custody industry. These are:

- legislation
- investors' desire to invest abroad
- custodian banks' expectation of profits from global custody activity
- technological developments.

These factors are discussed below.

Legislation

Since the mid-1970s, national legislation in most of the world's developed countries has played an important role in the growth of the global custody industry. Some legislation, but less than might be expected, has imposed statutory requirements on institutional investors – at both a domestic and global level – to place their clients' funds in the hands of domestic or global custodians or, more commonly, has created a self-regulatory framework where investors are encouraged to do this. Other forms of legislation have restricted share certificates and other valuable documents from leaving the country where they were issued, thus creating an automatic need for institutional investors moving capital to that country to use the services of a local bank to hold these valuable documents. The local bank is also likely to be used as a sub-custodian in other capacities.

Investors' desire to invest abroad

As we have seen, there is generally an expectation among investors that cross-border investments often have the potential to bring higher levels of return than those brought by purely domestic investments. We have also seen that such cross-border investments usually entail a higher level of risk, especially in emerging markets, and that custodians can make a major contribution to alleviate this risk

For reasons of sound common sense, investors will always invest where they have the best prospect for maximum return, given that they are prepared to accept the increased risk which, according to conventional investment theory, a desire for increased return always entails. It follows that some investors are likely to want to invest substantially – or entirely – in cross-border securities, and that even those with large domestic holdings are likely to want to have some cross-border investments in their portfolios. This, in fact, accurately describes what investors' attitudes towards cross-border holdings are in today's investment environment. There is no doubt that investors' desire to invest across national borders is a major force driving the development of the global custody industry. Furthermore, this interest in cross-border investments is only likely to increase in the future, especially as the fact that investors are constantly under pressure to gain better performance from their investments tends to make cross-border investments more popular. Many people or organizations, whose money the investor is responsible for investing, might blame the investor if there were no foreign investments in the portfolio and investment performance were less than spectacular.

Another key point to make here is that where global communications and global political relations are good, this tends to increase confidence in the viability of cross-border investments, and thus the amount of such investment. In practice, the relatively stable and generally healthy world economic scene that has prevailed since around 1980 – aided by governments which have on the whole been in favour of cross-border investment – has meant that foreign investment has continued to rise, both in absolute terms and as a proportion of the total fund available for investment. However, it can be argued that sometimes the apparent trend towards a global village being created – especially in the investment community – can give a misleading impression of the significant complications inherent in investing cross-border, especially in emerging markets. The truth is that, generally, many national securities markets in developing countries lag behind other elements of the infrastructure in terms of their progress towards Western standards of practice.

Custodian banks' expectation of profits from global custody activity

The belief on the part of many commercial banks that global custody represents an area where high profits are to be made, has also played a significant role in the growth of the global custody industry.

The basic reason for this belief is that global custody operation does not demand large amounts of risk capital to be put under potential jeopardy by banks. In this respect, global custody activity is greatly advantageous from a bank's perspective compared to traditional sources of profit such as personal loans and loans to corporations. Both of these clearly involve considerable amounts of risk, because no matter how well a bank checks the credit credentials of a customer, it can never be certain that the customer is always going to remain solvent.

Global custody, on the other hand, is fundamentally a service rather than a loan facility, and as such does not put large amounts of capital at risk. This is not to say that it does not require capital to be *spent* in order to operate as a custodian effectively, but this capital is expenditure rather than risk capital, and quite apart from being a tax-deductible business expense, it is seen as an investment by the custodian bank in its own operation.

Some risk capital *will* be involved; for example, the custodian will need to back certain trades with capital to ensure that they settle on time. Furthermore, global custody activity is certainly not without its risks from the custodian's perspective, because it will be liable to the customer if it makes a mistake or – which is hardly less common – fails to notify the customer of some important information (such as a corporate action notification) which it is contractually bound to handle. Even so, the level of risk should be considerably less than that which related to the bank's non-custody activities. Further information about the risk element of global custody is provided in Chapter 3.

Another major reason for banks having an expectation that global custody will be a major source of profits is that once they have a relationship with an institutional investor in place, there is every reason for them to believe that the relationship will bring them a regular income stream. To use a pleasing expression provided by a director of Lloyds Bank Securities Services, there is the expectation that global custody activity will provide an 'annuity income' which is regular and can be relied upon. Not surprisingly, in these highly competitive times when every bank has to struggle for market share, such income is extremely attractive. Furthermore, the credit risk exposure which global custodians have to their customers is very low, as their customers tend to be highly solvent and financially successful institutional investors who, by definition, have ample funds available.

It must be said, however, that events within the global custody industry have affected the perception of global custody as a profitable area of operations for a bank. Major mergers and shake-outs in the industry have led to a situation where there are today no more than about 20 major global custodians operating, worldwide. Of course, the fact that there have been mergers and shake-outs does not disprove the fact that there are substantial profits to be made. But it is indisputable that recent years have also seen considerable pressure on profits. Competitiveness among custodians has brought fee levels down to the lowest they have ever been, and indeed several shake-outs have stemmed directly from the fact that these low fee levels have made some players conclude that global custody is no longer a viable activity for them. At the same time, the role of technology in the industry has never been as important as it is today, and the need for global custodians to invest heavily in technology in order to keep up with their rivals is another reason why some have concluded that enough is enough and that the time has come for them to pull out of the business.

Technological developments

The opportunities for speed, accuracy, mass-volume processing and increased personalization of service, all of which are provided by technology, is undoubtedly a major driving force in the development of the global custody industry. Technology has provided custodians and their customers with enormously enhanced opportunities for not only automating their service but also for communicating with each other.

Technology is so important in this context that it deserves a chapter to itself, and Chapter 7 focuses entirely on technology. For the moment, it is important to state that technology is not only a major new factor in the operations of custodians but has also had a huge impact in many securities markets, which have frequently changed from an open outcry format to an automated format. Furthermore, technology has played and is playing a key role in the implementation of centralized securities deposit displays and electronic settlement systems which have had the effect of removing paper from the process.

THE GLOBAL CUSTODY INDUSTRY TODAY

Today, the international global custody industry is responsible for looking after assets worth about $24 trillion: which is a substantial part of the total capitalization of the major stock exchanges of the world. It is a burgeoning, highly competitive business in which custodians use a wide variety of human resources, commercial and technological infrastructures to maximize the appeal, efficiency and profitability of the services they offer clients, as well as a dynamic range of marketing techniques to demonstrate their particular skills and expertise to existing and potential customers.

As a result of the mergers and shake-outs of the past few years, the global custody industry has consolidated, with those global custodians left in the business generally being lean, fit, highly competent and well-financed. Regulation has played a role in speeding this consolidation; the industry is now subject to new levels of regulation which place an even greater burden on participants. Prices paid for global custody services are now again starting to show signs of rising a little compared with the past, and some custodians are enjoying enough success to feel able to refuse to compete on price in every case for every piece of business. They consider – not without reason – that there are abundant opportunities within the global custody business for real expertise to be displayed and that they have a right to insist on being paid properly for a top quality service. Which is fine, as long as the service remains top quality.

As for investors themselves, they will always be extremely demanding of their global custodians in terms of the level of ser-

vice the custodian provides. If their custodian – or one of their custodians – lets them down in this respect they may eventually
change them, although precisely how willing investors actually are
to change their custodians is something of a moot point. This is an
example of an occasion where grouping both institutional
investors and specialized investment management organizations
under the umbrella description of 'investor' is a little troublesome,
although usually it is a reasonable way to consider the industry. An
institutional investor will certainly care very much about the
quality of its custody service if the investor is managing its own
investments. However, if it is using a specialized investment manager it may not care who its contracted investment manager uses
as a custodian in a particular market but will be more concerned
simply about how the investment manager has performed. On the
other hand, some underlying clients are far from indifferent to
which custodian is being used and will enter into separate contracts and service level agreements with a custodian and will
instruct their fund managers to deal only with such custodians. As
so often in this industry, generalizations need to be tempered with
a respect for the likelihood that individual circumstances will
exhibit considerable individuality on the part of participants.

In an article about the global custody industry which I wrote in
the mid-1990s I commented that 'one of the undoubted attrac-
tions of global custody for commercial banks is that an investor has
every reason to want to stay with a global custodian as long as the
custodian is offering the requisite high level of service, because the
cost and inconvenience of transferring to another custodian is
likely to be high'. This point is still valid to some extent, mainly
because once an investor has set up an infrastructure for dealing
with one particular custodian, it is going to be onerous and time-
consuming to change this and changing it on a whim is not likely
to happen. For one thing, an investor which decides to change its
custodian will usually have to pay a fee to the custodian for depart-

ing, in order to compensate the custodian for procedures and infrastructures set up in order to help the investor. These fees, known as 'exit fees' can often run into many hundreds of thousands of dollars, although it must be pointed out that the new custodian who is coming on stream may, if the investor is large enough, offer to pay these charges to help the new business relationship get off to a good start.

Which is not to say that custodians can in any sense regard their clients as a 'captive audience' any more than a film director can regard a cinema audience as captive. Yes, there will inevitably be some forces of inertia at work: after all, they have gone to the cinema, sat down with their popcorn and are waiting to be entertained, but if the film is really tedious they will leave. Similarly, investors which are in bed with a particular global custodian will be willing to give it a chance. But global custodians need to keep their clients happy on a sustained basis if they are to continue to obtain business from them. One mistake or failing in the quality of service may not matter: several mistakes will, especially if the investor gets the impression that the custodian does not care particularly about the mistakes and is not over-eager to change procedures so that they do not happen again.

What *is* clear, however, is that for global custodians who are prepared to make the investment in technology and human resources necessary for success, the global custody business is a potentially major source of significant revenues, even with today's price levels that are much lower than those which prevailed early in the 1990s. Furthermore, global custody gives custodians the opportunity to forge long-term relationships with significant institutional investors or other investor clients whose other requirements can be met by the bank, often with even greater profitability.

The best worldwide survey of global custodians and custodians today is prepared by the magazine *Global Custodian*, which not only provides names, addresses and details of contact phone numbers for key personnel of all the world's global custodians and domestic custodians, but also uses a highly respected ranking system to assess the quality of the services provided. Not surprisingly, high rankings in the *Global Custodian* are greatly coveted and can be said to act as a means for improving levels of customer service throughout the industry. Readers seeking information about specific global custodians should refer to this magazine. There seems little sense in including this information in this book, because the global custody industry is still very much in a state of flux, and such material would rapidly become out of date. The same logic is behind my decision not to include any information about securities industry settlement conditions and other securities industry information relating to specific countries. Readers who seek this information should consult the superb handbooks and updates issued by the Zurich-based International Securities Services Association (ISSA). This organization owns the website www.issanet.org. It can also be contacted at the following address and telephone number: ISSA Secretariat, Union Bank of Switzerland AG, PO Box, 8098 Zurich, Switzerland. Tel: +41 1 235 7421.

CONCLUSION

In this chapter I defined key terms and emphasized the importance of the role of global custody in the bid for maximized fund performance and maximum quality of customer service. I emphasized that the importance of global custody derives substantially from investors' expectations that cross-border investments can bring a higher level of return than domestic investments. Finally, I considered the nature of the global custody industry and identified the major commercial banks as being the principal practitioners of that industry.

GLOBAL CUSTODY – THE SERVICES

3

INTRODUCTION

Newcomers to the global custody industry usually expect the services provided by global custodians to focus entirely or chiefly on the custody of assets; after all, this particular service is used as the name for the entire industry.

In fact, the breadth of services provided by global custodians is much more complex than that. Indeed the term 'custody' is nowadays completely inadequate to describe the range of services provided by global custodians. In many respects a much more accurate term would be 'international securities administration services'. But the term custody has stuck, partly for historical reasons (safe custody was the first global custody service offered) and also because it is a convenient term for summarising the entirety of all the services relating to the holding of assets.

Today's global custodians cover a range of services which are growing continuously broader and more complex. Understanding the nature of these services is essential for any investor, both because the investor needs to know what services are available, and also because the investor can only assess the range of services provided by a particular candidate custodian if it is aware of those which other custodians are offering.

We have already seen how competitive the global custody

industry has become. Faced with the need to be ultra-competitive at all times, it is hardly surprising that custodians are continually seeking to provide more services to their investors or clients, and to deepen the level of services provided to existing clients. As one experienced custodian told me: 'Providing the maximum level of service to one's investor clients not only increases your revenue, but also makes it more and more likely that the investor will come to depend on your services and will thereby remain with you for a long time.'

By virtue of being major commercial banks, global custodians are well-placed to provide a detailed range of services to investors relating to their foreign assets. That said, many global custodians, even now, are not fully alive to the need to employ specialists to provide different elements of the custody services, rather than simply generalist bankers who are mildly interested in working in the global custody department before developing their careers in other parts of the bank.

Readers would be right to suspect from this observation that many bankers do not regard a spell in the global custody department as a major source of career development opportunity. Even now, too many custodians both at a global and domestic level seem to insist on regarding global custody services as fundamentally dull and much too rooted in the back office to be glamorous or particularly interesting. As one highly experienced London-based global custody director told me: 'When you come down to it, global custody is really just a fairly tedious back office function.'

I emphatically disagree with this attitude, which seems to betray a lack of understanding of the breadth of activities which fall under the global custody banner. By the close of this chapter I hope the reader will share my views.

Another reason why the view quoted is a curious one is that the modern global custody industry is continually turning up examples relating to how the use of a good global custodian can greatly increase an institutional investor's competitiveness in the broadest sense. I examine this matter in greater detail in Chapter 4. In the meantime, I simply again point out the argument already discussed earlier in this book: that the Efficient Markets Hypothesis suggests that it is increasingly difficult for one particular fund manager to gain a performance edge over another without taking on undue risk, and that therefore any increase in revenue flowing to a fund which derives from good global custody practice must be extremely welcome. This view is, in fact, incontestable. As Roger Fishwick, a director of the UK's largest (by volume of assets managed) Prudential Portfolio Managers, told me:

> 'In my opinion there really is no doubt that a good global custodian can significantly increase the returns stemming from a fund and thereby make the institutional investor far more competitive. Not enough institutional investors recognize this; they ought to.
>
> From our own perspective, the facilities offered by the range of global custody services represent a prime element in our bid for maximum competitiveness and fund performance. Seeing global custody as a dreary back office function is foolish and indicates that there is something very wrong with the entire managerial attitude of the institutional investor. In fact, global custody provides abundant opportunities for investments to perform better and to generate more income.
>
> I suspect that the truth of the matter is that fund managers are only too pleased to attribute the successful operation and good performance of a fund under their control to their own managerial skills, and are unwilling to let themselves believe that global custody played an important role here.'

A good global custodian can greatly increase the chances of a fund being properly managed and handled, and make a significant difference to the revenue accruing from a particular investment. In order to understand this, we need to look at the various elements of the global custody service in detail. First, though, it is useful and instructive to look at an argument which is often voiced in the global custody industry today: that global custody services are being subjected to a process of commoditization.

THE COMMODITIZATION DEBATE

Commoditization is one of those terms much beloved of business commentators and management consultants who like to feel that they have their finger on the pulse of changing trends in business. Like many such terms, it is often used as a substitute for carefully investigating what is really going on, and has the added appeal that it gives users a fairly spurious sense that they know what they are talking about.

Commoditization is used to describe a process whereby traditional types of service and functionality are being provided by such a large number of suppliers, with those suppliers providing similar or identical types of service, that the service is supposed to be becoming standardized. If this were so, the only factor differentiating one service from another would be what the service costs.

The idea is that the services become, literally, 'commodities': rather like bags of refined sugar. Given that all the sugar is the same quality, and that the amounts of sugar in each package weigh the same, clearly the only differentiating factor between one supplier and another is the price. By extension, wherever a service or product is viewed as having become so standardized throughout the marketplace that providers are seen as only being able to compete on price, the term commoditization is invoked to describe the situation.

It must be said, however, that even where something as prosaic as sugar is concerned, commoditization might not be as accurate a description of the prevailing market conditions as might be imagined. For one thing, advertising is a powerful weapon in persuading consumers to view one brand of sugar as more desirable than another brand. Proof of the effectiveness of this strategy is that even though there are nowadays many supermarkets selling unbranded low-cost goods, mainstream supermarkets which sell more expensive branded goods continue to remain extremely popular.

Where sugar is concerned, it may be that the differentiating factor which advertising injects into a scenario is somewhat illusory, and certainly there cannot really be much difference in quality between refined sugar from a well-known brand name or one from a refiner which is less well-known. However, in the case of services which are inevitably complex, the situation is very different.

One would probably expect global custodians not to accept the idea of their services being in any sense commoditized, and they never do. The reason is not difficult to see. Once the global custodian (or domestic custodian) accepts that its services are commoditized, it is obliged to compete only on price, which is almost certain to be a severely retrograde step for it. Custodians much prefer to be able to claim a premium from the market for the quality of the service.

However, just because custodians are unwilling to accept the idea of commoditization, and, indeed, have a vested interest in not accepting that idea, does not mean that their thinking about it is unreliable. The truth is that it is eminently reasonable for custodians to maintain that commoditization does not apply in this case.

The only possible exception is in the area of highly routine services, settlement of familiar transactions such as domestic equity transactions for example, yet even here there is undoubted scope for the custodian to differentiate itself in the way it books on these transactions to its clients. In other, more complex areas of service, the difference between one custodian's level of service and another's is very considerable, and it makes no sense to regard these services as commodities in any sense.

If I am so opposed to the principle that commoditization applies to global custody services why do I include this section on it at all?

The reason is that many industry commentators claim that commoditisation does apply, but in my view this merely betrays a lack of knowledge on their part of the complexity of the global custody service, and of the breadth of the opportunities the service provides for personal expertise to make a mark.

As David Watson, director of marketing and business development at Lloyds Bank Securities Services – one of the UK's most eminent custodian organisations (although perhaps not a global custodians in the strictest sense, as its main domain is the UK) – told me:

> 'It's very misleading to talk about commoditisation in relation to the global custody business. Such an approach implies that the services provided by custodians are all very much the same, and this is not true. I would say that the global custody business is not about supplying commoditized services, but about the quality of the relationships between the custodian and its clients. For example, in our case I seek to have extremely personal relationships with our clients, which is why I take such effort to give clients precisely what they want. For example, when I book to a client over their holdings, I am careful to provide the book in the precise format I know the clients want, rather than in some standardized format which is common to all our clients. Describing the global custody business as one of commoditization of service is to neglect or overlook the extensive opportunities there are for one custodian to out perform another.'

I feel that David Watson's comments on this matter are reliable and in many respects represent what most global and domestic custodians think. Formal proof of the lack of true commoditisation in the industry is surely that institutional investors go to such great lengths to select global custodians who best meet their needs, and that many consultancies make a very good living from advising on this. If commoditisation really did apply, why would an institutional investor take such trouble to select a custodian according to a variety of criteria other than mere price? The discussion I provide later in this book on the whole business of selecting a global custodian, seems to me to represent the final word on this particular argument.

Turning now to the different types of global custody service, I start with a discussion of the difference between core global custody services and value-added services.

CORE AND VALUE-ADDED SERVICES

As the range of global custody services is so wide, it is useful and indeed necessary, to analyse it by categorising global services into *core* services and *value-added* services.

Precisely what constitutes core services and value-added services varies to some extent from one custodian to the next. The reason for this is that some custodians like to make much, in their marketing material, of the fact that they provide the widest range of services as core services rather than ones for which the investor is expected to pay extra. However, there is a general consensus that a certain class of services can usefully be categorized as core services, whereas another class of services can be categorized as value-added, because these services would be supplied by most custodians as something additional to the main global custody function.

I start the analysis by looking at core services, and then move on to services which may reasonably be described as 'value-added'.

CORE SERVICES

What exactly constitutes core services varies from one custodian to the next. However, there is something of a consensus that today's global custody industry regards core services as including all of the following:

- safekeeping and registration
- clearance and settlement
- income collection
- corporate action processing.

These four elements of the global custody service are usually known within the securities industry as Securities Movement and Control (SMAC) services. This term means that they relate to the fundamental process of handling transactions and controlling assets resulting from these transactions. It is true that there is something essentially arbitrary about limiting SMAC functionality to these four services, but this is a convention which most custodians are prepared to follow. SMAC services are now discussed in turn.

Safekeeping and registration

The safekeeping and registration service involves two principal components: the safe custody of all documentation relating to investments held and the registration of all assets held on the investor's behalf in the investor's name.

The safe custody of all documentation relating to investments held

The vast majority of items for which global custodians offer safe custody are share certificates and other relevant documentation. It is important to note that there is an increasing trend, especially in securities markets in developed countries, for share certificates and other documentation to be held in 'dematerialized' form, i.e. the certificates are stored electronically and manipulated by digital means. However, there remains in most jurisdictions a requirement for the original certificate still to be held in paper format, so the days of paper-based securities documentation are far from over. Note also that custodians sometimes become involved with holding tangible assets such as bullion, precious stones or even works of art. All items for which the custodian offers safe custody are usually held in a safe operated by the custodians within a strong room. Custodians generally have strict procedures governing the entry to these secure locations, with two individual members of staff typically being required and no single individual being permitted to examine safe materials held in the secure locations without another member of staff being available to monitor him or her. In the case of a safe, it is common for one member of staff to hold a key and for another member of staff to know the combination, with both the key and the combination being required to open the safe. This procedure clearly maximizes the likelihood that only bona fide people will gain access to the safe.

The registration of all assets held on the investor's behalf in the investor's name

This is typically done through the custodian setting up a nominee account in the investor's name. A nominee account is one which is set up to benefit a third party, whose authority is required for any transaction on that account. Note that in most developed countries, there is protection for the contents of nominee account under what is known as 'Trust Law', that is, law protecting the assets of an individual or a corporate entity held in trust. The crucial legal point here is that securities held in a nominee account are 'fungible', that is, they can be identified and attributed to a particular investor and there is no doubt about the ownership. On the other hand, cash is an asset which is *not* fungible, because it cannot readily be attributed to any particular person or organization other than in a purely numerical sense. As a result, cash is not usually protected by trust law, and investors have to accept that if the custodian became insolvent and ceased trading they would probably lose whatever cash was deposited with the custodian. This would not apply to securities held in a nominee account, which would be protected by trust law and would not be regarded as part of the custodian's assets at any time.

Two other important benefits to investors of having their assets registered under the investor's name in a nominee account are, first, that the assets can be audited by the investor's own auditors, who can treat them as assets of the investor, and second, that the investor can benefit from the publication of details of the holding in the annual book of companies which issue securities. Most countries have legal requirements that holdings above a certain percentage of a company's equity are publicized in this way, and such publicity is useful promotion for the investor, especially if it is a major institutional investor which wishes to be known as a reliable and discriminating participant in equity investment.

Clearance and settlement

Clearance and settlement are usually grouped together in any discussion of core global custody services because they are intimately related. They describe the process whereby a sale or purchase transaction of securities is completed.

Efficient clearance and settlement has always been an important element of any securities administration process, but has particularly come under a spotlight during the past ten years or so. It is of special importance when foreign assets are under consideration because the distance of foreign securities markets from the investor can cause clearance and settlement problems, and also because many foreign markets do not have as efficient clearance and settlement procedures as domestic markets. This is particularly true of foreign markets in developing countries.

Since around 1995, there have been significant advances in clearance and settlement procedures around the world. Before this date (I quote this year as an approximate guide rather than because it marks any particular development) two types of securities market tended to have clearance and settlement problems.

The first category were markets in developing countries, where the principal problem was frequently that the clearance and settlement system was not only strictly paper-based but also slow and often alarmingly inefficient. Developing markets have, generally, improved over the past few years, but some – notably India and Russia – are still extremely inefficient and are one of the primary reasons why global custody involving these countries always leads to a fair amount of risk. Later in this chapter I look at global custody services generally in relation to risk.

The other category of securities markets which often displayed problems in terms of clearance and settlement were long-established markets in developed countries, where the market had used an antiquated clearance and settlement procedure for so long that updating it was a fearsome task. Perhaps the best example of such a market was the UK, where until relatively recently the clearance and settlement procedure was based around a settlement day which arrived every two weeks. These settlement dates derived from the eighteenth century and were completely inappropriate in an age when there was a huge volume of securities transactions every single business day. The first attempt to upgrade the procedure resulted in a disaster. The London Stock Exchange's system, Taurus, went through a process of embarrassing delays and increased expenditure until it was formally scrapped in 1992, leaving the London Stock Exchange to write off a cost of £200 million. Taurus was replaced by the infinitely more successful Crest system. Crest is the book-entry dematerialized settlement system for corporate securities in the UK and Ireland. It went live on 15 July 1996 and provides modern, efficient and low-risk settlement to support the UK's international competitiveness. It is possible for investors to hold and transfer securities in electronic form in the UK and Ireland, if they wish to do so, but the option of retaining paper share certificates remains available. After the inauguration of Crest, there was a period of transition as holdings were transferred from paper to electronic form and settlement was moved from Talisman, the system previously operated by the London Stock Exchange, to Crest. This transition was completed in April 1997.

The one type of securities market which did not have settlement problems were the small securities markets in developed countries: markets which had abundant know-how and financial resources to facilitate rapid and smooth automation. For example, Scandinavian markets had little problem in automating the clearance and settlement function and by the early 1990s had in most cases done so. The trading volumes on these markets was not large and there was plenty of money available for the task. I remember visiting the Oslo Stock Exchange in 1989 to use their new automating system (which included a clearance and settlement function), and how efficient, meticulous and smooth the operation of the exchange was.

Why is efficient clearance and settlement so important for investors? The reason is that there is a clear link between the efficiency with which clearance and settlement is handled, and the overall competitive benefits to investors. In practice, a percentage of all trades in almost all markets fail to be settled, and this also creates risk for investors. On a more mundane level, efficient clearance and settlement is essential for investors for the following three reasons.

1 The sooner the investor is credited with the proceeds of the sale of an investment, the better this is for its cash-flow and revenue.
2 Similarly, since the investor clearly thought the purchase of the securities in question was a good idea, the sooner the investor owns the securities and can therefore qualify for interest and dividend (depending on the nature of the security) the better.
3 It is generally better for the investor's entire administrative

operation if the clearance and settlement of all its transactions takes place with maximum efficiency. This is especially important where the institutional investor is buying the securities on behalf of a major client such as a corporation or a pension fund, as the client will want the transactions to be resolved and to keep its books in order.

It is therefore essential that the custodian can offer it clients a clearance and settlement activity which provides maximum efficiency in terms of:

- accuracy of settlement
- speed of settlement
- the relaying of revenue deriving from sales to the investor
- rapid completion of purchases
- minimization of failed trades.

When, in the early 1990s, I started devoting a fair amount of my time to writing about global custody, I commented that efficient clearance and settlement are 'easier said than done'. This was a reasonable comment in view of the (then) fairly recent disaster of Taurus, and the fact that many countries' securities settlement systems were inefficient and left a great deal to be desired. The case that the recommendations made in March 1989 by the International think-tank on international affairs, the Group of Thirty (G30), were still largely unimplemented. These recommendations, while having no statutory force, were nonetheless held in great esteem by the financial community from the outset. The G30 had accurately predicted that as there was considerable concern within the international securities industry about inefficiencies of clearance and settlement, the industry would greatly respect a stand being taken on the issue by an influential international body.

It is not necessary to list the G30's recommendations here in full as they have to a considerable degree been implemented by many countries and are widely regarded as targets for implementation by others. Suffice it to say that the G30 strongly argued a case for nine different recommendations, of which the three most important can be regarded as a recommendation that Delivery Versus Payment (DVP) should be employed as the method for setting securities transactions; that a process of 'rolling settlement' should be adopted by all markets with a target of settlement of T+3 (i.e. all transactions settled three days after the trade date); and that securities lending and borrowing should be encouraged as a way of speeding the settlement of securities transactions.

The final point to make about settlement is to re-emphasize that there is a clear trend throughout the world to move towards shorter settlement cycles, and that custodians themselves are playing a key role in encouraging the continuance of this trend.

Income collection

Income collection is, for very obvious reasons, an essential core element of the global custody service. After all, the entire purpose of the investment is the income or capital growth deriving from it, and while some investors may be far more interested in capital growth than income, there is no such thing as an investor who is not at all interested in income, at least as far as securities investments are concerned.

Income deriving from investments varies according to the nature of the investment. In the case of bonds or fixed interest investments, the income is normally paid once or twice yearly. It is typically expressed as a per annum percentage rate before deduction of tax and is often referred to as the coupon. Collecting such income is usually fairly straightforward, given that the custodian has a local representative who knows when the income is due and can ensure that it is paid direct to the investor once it has been collected. In the case of highly rated bonds, such as government bonds in the major financial nations, income on bonds is effectively certain and usually paid automatically. In the case of government bonds in less well-established nations, payment of the income may depend on the political and academic climate and the representative may need to ascertain what the likelihood is that the income will be paid. Similarly, income deriving from corporate bonds will only be certain if the corporation in question is a highly rated one; otherwise income may not be certain or may be paid late. In any event, a local representative bank will have an important role to play in ensuring that the income is made available and, if there are going to be any problems with the coupon being paid, making sure that information about what is happening is relayed promptly to the investor.

Income deriving from equity investment consists of dividends paid by the corporations issuing the equity. These dividends will be the profit (if any) which the corporation has available for distribution to shareholders, who, after all, own the company.

Income collection places a heavy burden on custodians, because in order to do the very best job here they need to keep in touch with the affairs of the corporation in question, and they need to ensure that dividends are relayed to the investor as soon as they are paid. Many investors – especially large ones with plenty of financial influence – are able to conclude agreements with their custodians which stipulate when the dividend must be paid and will require the custodian to pay the dividend itself if it is late in collecting the money. Where a holding is substantial, the dividend payments can also be substantial and no custodian is going to survive in today's highly competitive market unless it can offer a superb and entirely (or almost entirely) error-free income collection service.

Obviously, where foreign holdings are concerned, the income collection problems are going to be more serious and this is particularly true of investments in emerging markets. In the latter case, the local representative bank or branch of the global custodian may need to chase income before it is paid and will almost certainly have to deal with a poor infrastructure. In this situation the custodian plays an even more crucial role in harvesting the income; a fact reflected in the much higher costs of carrying out custody requirements in emerging markets than in developed markets.

Income is usually paid into a nominee account, which the custodian holds on behalf of the investor. These nominee accounts are almost always held in the currency of the country where the investment itself is held, with the only exceptions being countries where the currency is not stable or where it is not easily converted, in which case it is likely that the custodian will want to convert it as soon as feasible and hold it in a nominee account in a more acceptable currency, which will typically be the investor's domestic currency.

The income which the investor can expect the custodian to collect on its behalf is known as 'assured income' and will usually be described as such in the service agreement between the investor and the custodian. This income is fundamental not only to the success of the investment process but its collection is also fundamental to the success of the custody relationship. Such agreements usually stipulate a day on which the income should be credited to the investor's account.

It might be imagined that all custodians would credit the income to the investors' accounts on the same day, but in practice there are some custodians that are prepared to offer the crediting of the income to the investor's account on the day when the income is due, even if this is not the date when the custodian actually received the money. In practice, there is usually a delay before the custodian does receive the money, with the delay being caused, for example by a hold-up from the government or corporation involved in sending the money or delays with the post. Some custodians are prepared to guarantee the payment of income to the investor on the due date whatever the situation as regards the actual receipt of the income. Clearly, some custodians do involve themselves in risk when they offer this service.

In the case of pension funds, income collection becomes even more important because the income from the investment will be used to fund liabilities which the pension fund will have towards its pensioners. Naturally, the custodian's role in this case becomes even more important. Note that pension funds usually keep a proportion of their assets in reliable government bonds in order to ensure that the income is received without fail on the due date and will be available for distribution to pensioners. Some pension funds hold assets in an account from which the distribution can subsequently be made.

Corporate action processing

The final element of the SMAC service is the monitoring, processing and relaying to investors of details of a wide range of 'corporate actions' taken by the foreign corporations in which the investor holds equities.

Of the four main elements of the core global custody service, corporate actions offer the highest likelihood of things going wrong. The reason is that whereas safekeeping and registration, clearance and settlement and income collection are all essentially *reactive* processes, that is, they require the custodian to react to some process that will either already have been initiated, or is being initiated by a third party, corporate actions require the custodian to maintain a vigilance which has to be open-ended, that is, there are no effective limits to it.

Why is this the case? The reason is that corporate actions are actions initiated by corporations in whose equity (or other stock) the investor has invested; *corporations which are not always very good at communicating the results of these corporate actions to investors.*

41

This is a real problem for custodians, because most will be working to a service contract which requires them to compensate investors if some benefit accruing from a corporate action is overlooked by the custodian and the investor is consequently not given the opportunity to benefit from the action, in other words, the custodian is responsible.

In practice, corporate actions represent a major area of potential risk for custodians, because there are so many opportunities for custodians to overlook important corporate actions which could bring benefits to clients, and to have to pay compensation as a result. This is particularly true of any corporate action which carries with it some kind of deadline by which the investor has to notify a certain intent if a particular benefit is to be obtained. For example, rights issues normally come with a date by which the right must be taken up if the shares in question are to be bought at the (usually) advantageous price. There have been many examples of custodians having to go into the market to buy shares at a (usually) less advantageous price in order to compensate the investor for a missed opportunity. I look at the entire question of the risk which a custodian bears on a client's behalf later in this chapter.

Typical corporate actions include announcements of:

- dates and times of annual general meetings (AGMs) and extraordinary general meetings (EGMs)
- scrip issues (i.e. the issuing of gratis stock to stockholders in some proportion to their existing holdings)
- rights issues (i.e. the creation of a right by an existing stockholder to buy more stock at what is usually a favourable rate)
- size and frequency of dividend payouts
- mergers and acquisitions
- initiation and/or response to takeover bids
- details of stock splits
- stock option plans

- voting opportunities relating to major decisions which the corporation has to take.

It cannot be overemphasized that *all* corporate actions are important, because they so directly concern the organizations in which investors hold stock. Rights issues and scrip issues are particularly valuable, as they constitute a way of increasing a stockholding either at no cost at all (in the case of scrip issues) or at a favourable cost (in the case of rights issues). Where an investor's holding is substantial, these corporate actions can be immensely valuable.

It follows that monitoring and processing corporate actions is a vital element in the work that custodians undertake for their clients. Extensive local resources and local market knowledge are required to discharge the responsibility. An investor that is seeking to win a competitive edge from its use of global custody must seek a custodian that has proven ability in providing a first-class corporate action service.

Another important point here concerns the business of casting votes at AGMs and EGMs. One of the most fundamental attributes of equity (ordinary share stock) is that it conveys voting rights in the affairs of the organization issuing the equity. Under most national jurisdictions, foreign holders of equities can vote on all matters which would usually be decided by shareholders.

The large scale of most institutional investments in a corporation usually means that the voting powers of institutional investors are substantial, in many cases far outweighing the voting powers of smaller, private investors. However, few institutional investors or other large investors are able to attend meetings organized by foreign corporations for voting purposes.

In the past, some investors accepted the impossibility of attending voting meetings and did not take up their voting opportunities. Other investors may have believed that even if they took the trouble to vote, their votes would not make any significant difference. This somewhat lackadaisical attitude towards taking up voting opportunities is rapidly being replaced by a realization that an investor who neglects the opportunity to vote on the actions of corporations in which it holds equities is behaving irresponsibly.

As is often the case, within the international securities business, this change of attitude originated in the US, where the value of 'proxy voting' as an important part of the assets resulting from foreign investments – rather than as an irritating chore – is now firmly recognized. Proxy voting refers to the process of casting a vote without physically attending the AGM or EGM in question. Proxy voting is usually accepted by post, although in some national jurisdictions, investors' authorized representatives are required to attend the meeting in person.

As one can imagine, a large equity holding confers important opportunities to influence the corporate governance of a corporation, and the need for large investors to make use of these rights and thereby play an often significant – if indirect – role in the management of the organization is now accepted throughout the international securities industry. There has been a distinct change of attitude in this respect over the past ten years or so, as in the past these voting rights were often ignored. Today, most institutional investors around the world take up their proxy voting rights, with US investors being particularly diligent in this respect.

This change in attitude is regarded by many US investors and custodians as originating with the US Department of Labor, which in the spring of 1988 stated that trustees of pension funds governed by the US Employment Retirement Income Security Act 1974 (ERISA) have a fiduciary duty to address matters of corporate governance. The department was in effect saying that trustees must take their proxy voting responsibilities seriously and exercise them.

The Department of Labor's decision, far from being a fickle ruling which involves investors in yet another administrative complication, makes good sense. The days when corporate voting related only to issues which would be passed at the meetings as a formality are fading fast and in many countries are already gone. Aggressive corporations – hungry for market share in an increasingly global, complex and highly dynamic business environment – frequently need to ask shareholders to vote on crucial matters relating to the impact which the corporation can make on its marketplace, the composition of the board of directors and their remuneration, and scrip and rights issues and all other consequences of holding shares.

Most important of all from the investor's perspective is the need to vote on the response to takeover bids. However, even less momentous decisions can have a significant effect on stock price. Many corporate matters which have sometimes been regarded by corporations and investors as formalities are nowadays matters which are subject to intense debate.

In the UK, for example, there has in recent years been considerable concern among many institutional investors and smaller investors that some directors of corporations are being remunerated excessively, with high salaries and large bonuses being paid, sometimes even if the corporation performs relatively poorly. As a result, there is now extensive debate in the UK about the contractual terms under which directors ought to be engaged. Voting rights give investors considerable say in how these and other issues should be resolved.

Most or all of the decisions on which an investor can vote will have an impact on the value of the corporation's stock, sometimes a significant impact. An investor who does not make arrangements for voting on these matters could be said to be behaving with some irresponsibility in relation to its investments, with this level of irresponsibility being correspondingly higher (as will usually be the case) when the investments are held on behalf of others.

Although the new emphasis on taking up voting opportunities

applies to stocks held in the investor's own country as much as stocks held abroad, the principal challenge to investors is the question of how to handle voting opportunities arising outside the investor's own country. In almost all cases where foreign investments are held, the investor must exercise a proxy vote: that is, a postal vote made without actually attending the meeting. This principle applies with particular force in Japan, where most of the annual general meetings tend to be held within the same few days, making it almost impossible for even the most assiduous local investor to attend all the meetings, let alone an investor based thousands of miles away.

Bearing all this discussion of corporate actions in mind, it follows that a global custodian must, if the investor is to extract the maximum competitive advantage from the arrangement, be able to provide a comprehensive, reliable, accurate and – above all – *timely* service to relay details of corporate actions to the investor. As for the proxy voting service which the custodian provides to the investor, the investor will only obtain the highest level of competitive advantage from the service if it offers certain important features. Incidentally, when written information is provided by the custodian to the investor, the investor is entitled to expect that this will be supplied by the custodian in the investor's own language.

The corporate action reporting and monitoring service should offer these features:

- coverage of all territories where the investor is interested in investing, including major markets and emerging markets;
- all types of corporate actions to be covered, with the custodian advising the investor of those which are of particular importance;
- provision of all information which the investor needs to make fully informed voting decisions;
- timely and accurate details of proxy voting opportunities, and

clear, jargon-free explanations of the issues at stake in the voting process;

- the taking up and enactment of selected proxy voting opportunities, even in the most difficult territories, including the execution of legal documents;

- the custodian can – when necessary and authorized by the client – attend meetings to represent the client's interest, and to influence proceedings to the client's advantage.

This concludes the survey of core global custody services. I now move on to looking at value-added services.

VALUE-ADDED SERVICES

A value-added global custody service is any service which a global custodian does not include as part of its core services. This is a less tautological and unhelpful definition than might be imagined, because most custodians do indeed offer a slightly different range of core and value-added business services, with there being a clear trend in favour of a custodian including a wide range of services as core services.

As this fact might imply, there is no widely accepted definition within the global custody industry of what a value-added service is. Competition between custodians is continually broadening the range of services they offer, and even within the lifetime of this report there are likely to be new services being provided. The point is that a custodian is perfectly entitled to offer its investment clients any service which they are likely to need, if by offering the service the custodian is likely to provide more client satisfaction.

In practice, the following are the most commonly offered value-added services:

- cash management
- country information provision
- investment accounting and reporting
- performance measurement
- performance attribution
- assistance with regulation and compliance
- securities lending
- tax reclamation
- unit trust trusteeship

These services are considered in detail below.

Cash management

David Watson of Lloyds Bank Securities Services describes cash management as: 'An area where one custodian can increasingly gain an edge over another if it is properly geared up to handle this.'

The point is that all investment portfolios are bound to contain some surplus cash at any given time. This is not like the cash in one's pocket; it can be very substantial. It usually derives from the simple fact that there is always a case for keeping some cash back to exploit any investment opportunities which might arise. Furthermore, if the investor has just sold some securities it is very likely that the funds deriving from this sale will not yet have been invested in other securities and there will therefore be a cash holding as a result.

The custodian's role is ultimately not so much to help maximize fund performance as to maximize the efficiency with which the investor's assets and money are handled. In practice, there is no reason why the investor should not hold the cash itself. However, the custodian – being a commercial bank – will be ideally placed to know what to do with this cash and to get the best return for it.

An important additional point to make is that the larger the cash deposit the better the rate of interest, and a custodian will typically have many investors who will all have spare cash. This cash can consequently be pooled together and put on deposit at the most favourable rate, with the interest deriving from this being distributed among the investors in accordance with the proportion of the cash that was theirs.

Custodians generally have their own rate for cash deposits and will need to be highly competitive in this respect. There are also special investment funds where cash can be placed for a short term (typically varying from one day to around three months). Again, these funds need to offer a highly competitive rate.

What is incontestable is that cash must be put to work right away, otherwise the investor is simply losing money on it and may in some cases be able to claim compensation from the custodian.

Where the cash is placed on deposit with the custodian, this cash is not strictly speaking managed by the custodian (who, I must emphasize, is not in the business of fund management) but is rather being handled to the investor's greatest benefit. A good custodian will be able to offer its clients a range of cash deposit options varying from interest-bearing current accounts to active cash deposits using the money markets. The particular avenue an investor chooses will depend on how rapidly it expects to need access to the cash.

The cash sums available for custodians to invest on their clients' behalf often amount to many millions of pounds. Clearly, the better the return that the custodian can achieve on investors' cash balances, the better the overall return on its investment, and the greater the competitive advantage which the investor has a chance of enjoying.

If the investor is to enjoy maximum benefit from cash management, the custodian must be able to provide all the following services:

- pay credit interest on sterling and currency call accounts;
- arrange cash sweeps to high-interest dividend accounts;
- place funds on deposit with the bank's treasury department on behalf of the investor;
- make markets in appropriate currencies where the market-making facilities are not already available;
- offer active deposit-placing facilities in all the markets applicable to the investor.

In the latter case, when the custodian is actively placing deposits, this arrangement should involve the investor and custodian agreeing in advance the parameters for managing the surplus cash. Typically the investor will be required to nominate the deposit-takers it finds acceptable, and the amounts, currencies and duration of the deposits to be placed with a particular counterparty.

Naturally, the investor must be completely satisfied at all times that the banks taking the deposits are reliable and creditworthy. The investor is well advised to restrict its banks to those with a top-level credit rating.

Another useful credit standard is the International Bank Credit Agency (IBCA) rating, which varies from one to five, with banks graded one being regarded as the best risk. This rating is substantially influenced by the perception of the likelihood of the national bank stepping in if the bank in question were to experience a failure. In the UK, for example, the IBCA rating is considerably influenced by the estimated likelihood of the Bank of England intervening to save the bank in question from collapse. At present, only two top UK clearing banks have a one grading by IBCA. Incidentally, note that the IBCA rating of Barings Bank prior to its demise was four.

Country information provision

Throughout their operation, custodians must at all times remember that they are not fund managers and must not advise on the desirability or otherwise of an investment. The reason for this strict demarcation is not so much because custodians have no idea about whether an investment is likely to be a good one or not, but because they must avoid possible conflicts of interest. If, for example, a global custodian had just appointed a sub-custodian in the Czech Republic, the custodian would hardly be a completely objective source on the question of whether the Czech equities market represented a good investment area, because the custodian would want the business.

Even though this demarcation between the custody and investment management function should be closely followed, custodians are perfectly entitled to pass on information to their clients on developments in different countries where the client is investing. It is almost impossible for a particular investor who is undertaking considerable cross-border investment, to monitor developments in all the countries where he or she holds investments. It would be difficult to do this even if the investor worked at investment full-time; for many investors this is not the case and they certainly need the custodians assistance here. For example, high net worth private investors with substantial foreign investment holdings are likely to be far too busy running their businesses or pursuing their careers to monitor developments in countries where they are investing.

Global custodians, on the other hand, are perfectly placed to monitor developments because they will be in constant contact with their foreign agents, whether these are their own foreign branches or sub-custodians they appoint. The custodian has a duty to report to the investor details of developments which may have an adverse or positive effect on the investments and most global custody service contracts nowadays contain a provision for such information to be relayed. Indeed, many global custodians take a pride in their expertise in all the countries where they hold assets and are only too keen to pass on the information they know.

Typical kinds of information which an investor will want to know are:

- significant economic developments (e.g. increases in the interest rate, details of inflation, information about balance of payments)
- stock market developments, especially sudden hikes or reductions in the stock exchange index
- major political developments, especially election results and details of political crises
- details of any regulatory rulings which may affect certain industrial or commercial sectors.

Naturally enough, country information is especially important where it concerns an emerging market which might, in any case, be expected to feature a relatively unstable economic and political background. Custodians offering a service in emerging markets usually are particularly vigilant regarding developments; a fact usually reflected in the fees they charge for this service.

Investment accounting and reporting

This service involves the custodian providing the investor with all types of data relating to the accounting and current status of the portfolio. The information is increasingly provided electronically, although as an alternative to, rather than substitute for hard copy information.

Investment accounting reports usually include all the following information:

- details of all investments currently held by the investor, with current valuations;
- summary of realized gains/losses on securities bought and sold, and on foreign exchange transactions;
- summaries of holdings by asset classification, industrial sector and geographical location;
- cash journals;
- income accrual statements;
- cash and asset reconciliations;
- consolidated reporting across managers, i.e. a report on the performance of each manager;
- reporting on the '3 per cent of issued capital' (this refers to the fact that some pension funds, such as those in the UK are – for reasons of investor protection – not allowed to hold more than 3 per cent of their assets in one particular stock).

The quality of investment accounting and reporting is essential to investors as it lets them keep track of the current performance of funds and also lets them see which assets they currently hold. Furthermore, the tracking of financial performance across the fund's investment managers allows the investor, if it wishes, to switch assets from a worse-performing manager to a better-performing manager.

The presentation of accounting and reporting information is not a trivial matter, because this should ideally be tailored to the investor's precise requirements and can bring great benefits to the investor if it is. For example, a pension fund may want its reports to look somewhat different from the kind of reports favoured by a private investor.

Unfortunately, many investors still persist in supplying accounts and reports which are laid out in a dull, unattractive format, with little concession made to the investor's desire for clarity and appeal in this information. A pension fund may be administered by people who are not themselves investment specialists, and if the report is not easy to read, it may be difficult for the pension fund to understand what is really going on. Indeed, custodians sometimes appear to forget that investors are not always necessarily financial professionals, and cannot invariably read written documentation with ease when it is laid out unattractively. An investor has every right to expect that custodians should present this information clearly.

Finally, custodians must also remember that their clients will often be passing the reports onto their *own* clients. This will typically apply where an investor is an investment management organization which specializes in handling corporate funds and pension funds. The same logic as in the preceding paragraph also applies here: these funds will frequently not be run by investment specialists and the reports must therefore be clear and readable.

The regularity of these reports will depend on what the client wants. They are usually prepared on a monthly or quarterly basis, but some investors may prefer them to be fortnightly or even weekly. Obviously the custodian should comply with the client's wishes in this respect.

Performance measurement

As its name suggests, this service provides the investor with detailed information about the actual performance of the funds which the custodian handles on the investor's behalf. Providing a performance measurement service is nowadays regarded as an almost essential value-added function of a custodian, and most will aim to offer such a service if it is feasible to do so.

It is clear that a custodian is in a particularly good position to provide performance information by the very fact that they will be in touch with all the different fund managers looking after a particular fund (I am talking here about institutional investors who use a number of fund managers). Global custodians can consolidate performance information and present it in whatever way their client wishes. Fund managers are naturally keen to know about performance as they can use good performance in advertising material and marketing literature.

Performance measurement information is very valuable and not as easily come by as might be imagined. Custodians will guard it jealously. Some will handle the actual collation of information themselves, others may delegate this to a specialized performance measurement organization, such as the WM Company.

Clearly, to re-emphasize a point made above, performance measurement is extremely important for the end-user investors because it allows them to monitor how well fund managers are doing on a monthly basis and to switch funds to higher-performing managers if they wish.

Performance attribution

This is a relatively new service and many custodians do not yet offer it, although there is every indication that more will do so in the future.

Performance attribution takes performance measurement a step further by seeking to *attribute* performance to a particular source. It is true that in some cases an investment manager may have some inherent skill which lets them consistently turn in a good performance, but modern portfolio theory suggests that this will not usually be the case, i.e. that few fund will be able to turn in a consistently good performance. Instead, it is likely that the higher performance will stem from some particular investment technique or from a particular geographical location or industrial sector which the fund manager is favouring.

The point of performance attribution is to identify the source of the (usually better than average) performance and thereby give the investor the opportunity to switch funds to that particular source. For example, if fund manager X has invested significantly in ME high-growth equities, especially those in the electronics and biotech sectors, and has thereby gained a good performance, while fund manager Y has gained only a middling performance by investing in UK blue chip equities, the investor will want to know about this. It does not necessarily mean that the investor will switch all his or her funds to ME high-growth equities, but he or she will appreciate knowing what is causing the higher performance. As with performance measurement, custodians are ideally placed to consolidate information on this matter from all the different fund managers acting on behalf of a particular investor.

Assistance with regulation and compliance

This service involves the custodian advising the investor on the following matters.

1 Various aspects of conforming to official regulations relating to the making and handling of investments. Every investor operates under a particular regulatory authority. For example, in the UK most investors are regulated by the Investment Management Regulatory Authority. The regulatory organization will require that certain procedures and protocols are followed by the investor, and the custodian is ideally placed to advise on whether these are being followed, and indeed to alert the investor to any points which are not being adhered to.

2 Certain in-house rules which the investor organization may implement relating to the conduct of investment and, in most cases, restricting investments to particular categories. As with general regulations, custodians are ideally placed to assist with monitoring compliance with in-house rules. Indeed, they are often, paradoxically, better placed to do this than the investor

itself, as the custodian will know exactly what each fund manager is doing.

Securities lending

In today's investment community, traders frequently 'sell short' in a particular security in order to exploit an opportunity for profit which arises at short notice. When this occurs, they frequently need to borrow securities to make up the shortfall and ensure that the transaction is completed satisfactorily.

In the majority of cases, the source of these securities are institutional investors that hold them in their portfolios. The process of securities lending involves the securities being lent out for a particular period in exchange for collateral, in particular cash or some other readily liquid asset, typically deposited with the lender when the borrowing is initiated.

Selling short is not the only reason why a stock might need to be borrowed. Sometimes the borrower needs the stock to settle a failed trade, or to participate in arbitrage activity.

Securities lending was actively encouraged by the G30, when it issued its recommendations for settlement procedures in March 1989. The G30's eighth recommendation began by saying 'securities lending and borrowing should be encouraged as a means of expediting the settlement of securities transactions'.

Today, securities lending is an accepted and increasing practice within most major financial markets, although it is not yet allowed in every market, especially some emerging markets without adequate infrastructures for ensuring that the borrowing can be handled with complete security.

Global custodians are increasingly offering securities lending as a key value-added service. They are doing this for two reasons. First, it is clearly in their interests to help investor clients maximize the revenue which investors derive from their assets. If this revenue is maximized, the investor is likely to have a high level of satisfaction with the custody service and give more business to the custodian, or simply retain the custodian in the future. Note also that in some cases revenue from securities lending activity can pay partially or even completely for the custody service. This is particularly the case with large institutional investors who do not practice a great deal of cross-border investment and who have substantial securities holdings. Second, by the very nature of their activity, global custodians are perfectly placed to manage securities lending activity for their clients. Custodians have knowledge of the range of investors' holdings and the availability of these holdings for lending at a particular time and for a particular period. Equally importantly, the custodian will have access to the investor's entire pool of stock, and will have the size and overall financial strength to provide guarantees for the collateral for the loans. Custodians should also be well-placed to negotiate the best deal in the marketplace for the investor, and also to identify potential lending opportunities.

This last point is especially important. In many financial markets the supply of securities for lending at any time considerably outstrips the demand. In the UK, for example, it is estimated that at any one time there is in the region of £60 billion of securities available to lend, while the borrowing requirement is about £3.5 billion. Clearly, the range of contacts which the custodian has among lenders and borrowers, coupled with its credibility as a manager of lending activity, will maximize lending opportunities for the investor.

Securities are lent either on an 'on call' basis, meaning they can be drawn at short notice (typically two to three days) whenever required, or else lent on fixed terms, which usually vary from overnight to about three months.

Revenue from securities lending comes to investors in the form of commission on the loan. The commission will vary both in relation to the size of the loan and – more significantly – in relation to the level of demand for the security in question, with the demand being directly proportional to the lack of availability of the security.

Commission is paid in terms of 'basis points' with one basis point being 0.01 (i.e. 1/100 of a per cent). The usual range of commission paid varies from about ten basis points (0.1%) to 200 basis points (2%) of the current market value of the stock which forms the loan.

Finally, note that the custodian bank's creditworthiness is a factor in the successful completion of the securities loan. The reason is that securities lending involves an actual transfer of title of the securities and therefore the custodian bank needs to have the credit rating and credibility to ensure that the lender is confident with the security of the loan throughout the entire process. This explains why, where a global custodian uses a local agent bank, the securities lending process will be managed by the global custodian, which will usually have a better credit rating than the local bank, especially in emerging markets.

Tax reclamation

Tax reclamation is essentially a sub-set of income collection, but it is so important that it deserves to be seen as a value-added service and indeed is sold as such by many custodians.

Tax reclamation is necessary because most foreign countries deduct tax at source on dividend and other income payable on securities holdings. As investors will have to declare this income gross in their own country, they will be paying the tax twice if the tax is not reclaimed from the foreign country when it is deducted at source.

In practice, the task is not quite as difficult as it sounds, because double taxation treaties exist between most countries, allowing tax to be reclaimed on foreign earnings and only paid once at a domestic level. Of course, some investors deliberately use offshore accounts which have no tax liability anywhere. Using offshore accounts itself is perfectly legitimate; but not if the investor uses the account to hide income received from his or her domestic tax agency.

The tax reclamation service provided by global custodians is essentially an administrative service and involves the custodian liaising with the foreign tax authority locally and negotiating the return of the tax. Local liaison is almost always necessary because tax authorities are rarely geared up to deal with parties located abroad and usually require that the reclaimed tax is paid into a domestic account, such as one held by a sub-custodian bank.

Needless to say, procedures for tax reclamation are laborious and involve the completion of complex application forms in the language of the country concerned; a task difficult or impossible for a foreign investor who does not speak the language.

In practice, tax reclamation is handled by the sub-custodian (the foreign office of the global custodian) and managed by specialized staff who not only have expertise in this area, but also nurture good contacts with local tax authorities. In some countries (it would not be appropriate to say which) this process of nurturing contacts involves a certain amount of hospitality being given to the tax office staff in question, and there is no doubt that on some occasions the demarcation between hospitality and bribery starts to blur. However, in most countries where an investor is likely to want to invest money, there is a vigorous movement against such corruption, and there is every chance that global custodians should be able to avoid it to a considerable extent.

That said, there is no substitute for the custodian using an agent bank with real expertise in this area, because despite the progress being made within the international securities industry on such matters as standardization of securities numbering procedures and the streamlining and modernizing of national clearance and settlement procedures, it remains the case that tax reclamation is an area where inflexible national procedures conspire to inhibit progress in streamlining tax-related issues.

A global custodian offering a tax reclamation service needs to be familiar with all the following areas relating to tax reclamation in the country in question. These are listed below with related questions and comments.

'At source' relief

Is it possible for eligible foreign investors to benefit from the reduced rate(s) of tax to which they are entitled at the time of income payments (without any undue administrative burden being imposed)?

While larger investors obviously stand to gain the most financial benefit from incremental income earned on the funds which have been relieved from excess tax, the benefit accruing to the small investor from 'at source' tax relief arrangements should not be underestimated. This is because the individual amounts of tax relieved 'at source' may not be economic to claim retrospectively and may otherwise not be pursued.

Tax relief infrastructure

Are there properly structured procedures in place for claiming tax relief (whether by means of an 'at source' arrangement or by retrospective tax reclaim)? If so, are these procedures well documented?

Properly structured and documented tax relief procedures should act as a catalyst, enabling regulatory provision to be converted cleanly into practical tax relief. The absence of such an infrastructure will often result in uncertainty as to the competent tax authority's precise requirements. It is likely that effective resolution will add to the overall administrative burden, and delay the provision of tax relief.

Tax reclaim lead time

Where it is necessary to submit a tax reclaim application for excess tax deducted, will the competent tax authority make a refund payment within a reasonable period of time (for example, within four months of receipt)?

Clearly, the less time taken by the tax authority to review and approve tax reclaim applications, the more quickly the investor will receive the benefit of the tax relief or refund.

Centralized tax administration

Are claims for tax relief handled by a centralized tax administration?

From a tax perspective, a centralized tax administration for the handling of claims by foreign investors is usually a positive advantage. In the absence of a centralized body, claims for tax relief are usually made to the regional tax office which handles the affairs of the issuing entity. Unfortunately, the use of regional tax offices greatly increases the potential for inconsistency (between one tax office and another). Even where properly documented tax relief procedures are in place, variations in interpretation can still occur. The net result is often uncertainty of tax administration requirements.

Investor orientation

Does the competent tax administration orientate itself towards the needs of its 'customer' (the foreign investor)?

The common perception of a tax administration is that of an unwieldy bureaucracy. For many countries, this perception is unnecessarily pessimistic. If approached in a professional way, and if the investor or the custodian shows a willingness to co-operate with the tax authority's procedures, many tax authorities are helpful. However, there remains a small minority of tax administrations that demonstrate little willingness to comprehend the nature of global investment and, in particular, the clear differences that exist between the global investor and his or her domestic counterpart. Such intransigencies will often manifest themselves in delayed (or denied) tax relief and in the imposition of inhibitory administrative burdens.

Special rulings

Is the competent tax authority prepared to consider applications for special rulings?

The eligibility (or otherwise) of most categories of foreign investors to tax relief is usually clearly defined. However, for certain categories of investor, the position is less certain. Such investors may include collective investment vehicles which are not in themselves the legal owner of the underlying securities. For investors such as these, the ability to obtain tax relief may be contingent upon a special ruling being agreed with the competent tax authority. It is therefore vital that the tax administration concerned be prepared to make such a ruling. Otherwise a decision must be made, either:

- not to progress claims for tax relief; or
- to present such claims, together with the relevant facts, to the tax administration in the hope that the claims will not subsequently be rejected (with possible retrospective effect). The possibility of retrospective claw-back will be of particular concern to certain categories of investor, such as investment vehicles whose units are regularly priced (and where that price includes the value of tax relief claimed without prior tax authority approval).

Not surprisingly, most investors prefer to delegate their tax reclamation affairs to their custodians, which have representation, or their own offices, in the foreign country in question, and local staff who speak the language and who are likely to have experience of reclaiming tax from the same authorities for domestic clients.

Overall, the competitive potential of the tax reclamation service to the investor is immense. An investor who has access to a custodian that can provide a top-class tax reclamation service will have a major competitive advantage over investors that do not, or whose tax reclamation service is not particularly effective.

Unit trust trusteeship

Where the investor's activity involves the construction and marketing of unit trusts, it is often convenient for the unit trust to use the custodian as a trustee.

Using a custodian as a trustee of a unit trust will bring various advantages in terms of speed of communications, administrative efficiency and general expertise of the custodian. All these advantages will help towards winning the investor an edge in the highly competitive unit trust business.

CUSTODY RISK AND THE ROLE OF THE CUSTODIAN IN HELPING TO MANAGE THIS

The reader will now have an understanding of the nature of both the core and value-added global custody services. Certainly an understanding of these different types of service is essential for anybody planning on using the services of a global custodian or working within the global custody industry in any capacity. However, an understanding of the core and value-added services provided by custodians is only part of the story. It is also extremely important to understand that global custody activity involves the custodian taking on a considerable amount of risk.

Figure 3.1 illustrates what might be described as the custody risk matrix. It covers every aspect of custody and the risk that this activity entails. From the investor's point of view, it is essential that there is an understanding that working with any custodian – no matter how high-profile or successful – carries with it a certain amount of risk. This does not necessarily mean that this risk is ultimately all borne by the investor; indeed, this is rarely the case, because most custodians offer formal indemnities or other guarantees of compensation for any loss the investor suffers as a result of poor performance by the custodian or some actual case of fraud perpetrated by a member of the global custodian's or sub-custodian's staff.

Figure 3.1 Types of custody risk

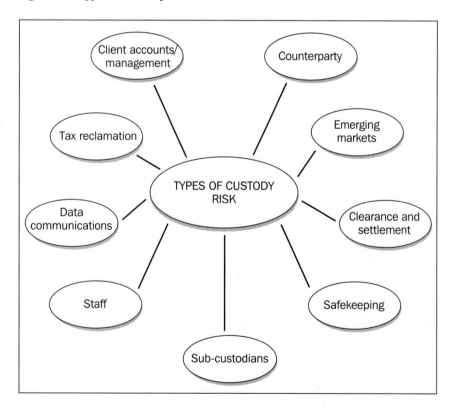

These indemnities or guarantees do give investors a considerable amount of protection, and not surprisingly, the extent to which the custodian is prepared to provide such indemnities is an important matter for negotiation when contracts are signed. Generally, custodians are aware that they need to provide some indemnity, but they will attempt to minimize this as far as is likely to be acceptable to the investor. Obviously, if the custodian provides too much indemnity it may be at a disadvantage from a financial perspective, and it will need to take out expensive insurance to guard against the indemnity being required. It may gain more business as a result of the higher indemnity, but its financial performance could be affected. Conversely, if the custodian does not provide adequate levels of indemnity, it will need to have a very good track record of performance to avoid losing business as a result.

This need for custodians to balance a willingness to provide indemnities with the requirement to operate cost-effectively means that many are starting to conduct their own internal risk audit to look carefully at what levels of risk are inherent in their operation. This will greatly assist with their ability to offer realistic indemnities which will be attractive to investors without involving the custodian in having to spend vast amounts on insurance.

However, it would be naive to suppose that custody risk is merely a matter of avoiding dramatic losses. The truth is that custody risk, like many types of risk, is ultimately a reflection of the overall efficiency of the custodian. Besides, by no means all types of custody risk can be insured against by the custodian. Deliberate fraud or malpractice by members of staff can be insured against, and so can staff incompetence or oversight, at least to some degree, but a full custody risk audit covers all areas of the custodian's operation which have the potential for a lower level of performance than would be desirable, and there is no way that every element of that low level of performance can be insured completely.

A custody risk audit is therefore doubly useful for custodians, as not only should it reveal areas of serious opportunity for loss due to fraud or malpractice, but it should also unearth areas of activity where overall efficiency could be improved. It is strongly recommended that any investor reading this should not enter into any contractual relationship with a custodian unless the custodian has tangible evidence that it has conducted an internal risk audit.

Looking in detail at Figure 3.1, the different types of risk are arranged so as to move by a logical process from the start of the transaction to the completed settlement and administrative process. Looking at the figure in a clockwise direction, the different types of risk, with accompanying comments, are as outlined below.

Counterparty risk

This is the risk that any counterparty used by their custodian incurs some liability, or fails in some other respect, and that the custodian may have to make good the liability or failure. It would cover such organizations as brokers, external markets and any other counterparty with which the custodian does business. It is a type of risk that is difficult to control. However, some insurance policies do allow insurance to be taken out against it.

Emerging markets risk

This covers all the areas of risk relating to handling assets held in emerging markets. It would have to cover unforeseen political and economic developments, as well as the inherent difficulties in dealing with markets whose infrastructures are, by definition, unlikely to be as sophisticated as in developed markets. Emerging market risk is always something of a thorny problem for global custodians because there is not much they can do about it apart from hiring the best local agents banks they can to look after their interests locally. The one optimistic note to sound is that the authorities in emerging markets are increasingly aware that poor infrastructure is a definite disincentive to foreign investors and so they are keen to do something about this.

Clearance and settlement risk

This is the risk that the transaction may either not be settled at all, or be settled late for some reason. It also covers failed trades. Even though, as we have already noted in this chapter, there is a definite move towards clearance and settlement systems becoming increasingly efficient and rapid, many markets still leave a great deal to be desired in this respect. Failed trades are always bad news for custodians and there seems no way that they can be guarded against completely. One definite positive move which a custodian can, however, take, apart from lobbying for improvements in clearance and settlement procedures in all the markets where it does business, is to make use of any opportunities to handle securities in dematerialized form, which tends to reduce the risk of failed trades and to speed up the process.

Safekeeping risk

This risk relates to the straightforward (but by no means necessarily simple) matter of actually holding the physical documents of title to the securities in question. Many of the world's securities markets accept securities processing based around a dematerialized or electronic document of title. However, safe custody of the physical documents is still necessary, and is a major part of what global custodians do. Formal safekeeping of documents is always going to be an area of risk for custodians and ultimately there is not a great deal they can do to eliminate this area of risk completely. Documents are normally kept in safes to which at least two members of staff have access and where no access can be allowed without both members of staff being present. As well as the security risk of the safe, there is often a risk that documents may be put into the safe and forgotten about. It is therefore necessary for a custodian to keep careful track of everything in its safe and have these details on-line for any staff members who may want them.

Sub-custodian risk

This is the risk that a sub-custodian fails to do what it is contracted to do. The whole process of selecting sub-custodians is always a complex one for global custodians, especially because in some markets it may simply not be possible to obtain a sub-custodian whose commercial practices and creditworthiness are as good as those of the global custodian itself. Sub-custodian selection and monitoring is always going to be a challenge for global custodians. Perhaps the best way of minimizing risk here is to ensure that the precise service standards expected of their sub-custodian are enshrined in the contract between the global custodian and the sub-custodian, with the sub-custodian being encouraged to use this contract as its working document. Furthermore, the sub-custodian should be able to provide indemnities or guarantees to the global custodian in the event of poor performance or actual fraud or malpractice.

Staff risk

This concerns incompetence, fraud or deliberate malpractice by the global custodian's staff. Obviously, there are many steps which a global custodian can take to minimize the likelihood of its staff letting it down. Proper training programmes, which should ideally include screen-based access to procedures so that the staff member always knows what needs to be done, can play a major role in preventing a mishap due to incompetence, and careful vetting of staff before appointing them can guard against staff malpractice or fraud. It is now accepted practice for custodian banks to undertake a check of a prospective staff member's personal credit record before appointing them, as a prospective recruit with a poor credit record may have financial problems that might lead them to commit some acts of fraud. Custodian banks usually also provide counselling services which can greatly help to prevent staff members' personal or financial problems which lead them to take part in fraudulent behaviour. Of course, these measures can never eradicate the possibility of such behaviour completely, which is why custodians need an insurance policy to guard against staff risk.

As we have seen, there are certain crucial areas of custody activity where there is a particularly strong potential for errors which can cost the custodian substantial amounts of money in having to compensate investors. This is particularly true of corporate action, where rights issues and scrip issues, if not properly notified to the investor or client in time, can lead to the custodian having to make redress to the investor. Rights issues and scrip issues have deadlines connected with them, and if the investor has not notified his or her requirements to the company in question by the time of the dead-line, it is likely that the benefits will be lost. The global custodian is, naturally, responsible for this notification and for chasing the investor to obtain details of what the investor wants. But the best remedy here clearly is to identify these areas of particular impor-tance in the custodian/investor relationship and ensure that at least two people are involved with monitoring the efficient and proper handling of the process. As with all types of custody activity, such vigilance is a much better solution than draconian punish-ment if the staff member does not do his or her job properly.

Data communications risk

This covers the risk of the custodian's own data communications, or a communications systems of its counterparties, not handling the transaction properly or making some kind of error. A proper computer security audit of the custodian's activities is an integral part of the overall risk audit, and the target performance of basic communications systems should always be a 100 per cent error-free operation. Furthermore, it is essential that messages sent via the data communications system feature both encryption and message authentication; the first prevents an unauthorized party from reading the message, the second checks that the message has not been tampered with during transit.

Tax reclamation risk

This is given as a separate area of risk because although it is ultimately part of the services which should be covered by staff risk, tax reclamation is such an important service that the custodian needs to pay special attention to the risks of the job being done inadequately. Insurance will not cover this; it is a matter of the staff involved doing the job thoroughly and following vigorous and rigorous procedures to ensure that tax is reclaimed at the earliest opportunity.

Client accounts/management risk

This risk relates to the handling of client accounts and the overall efficiency of how the custodian/client relationship is managed. There is not much that can be done to insure against possible problems here. However, there is a definite risk if the custodian does not fulfil its obligations: the risk of the investor moving to another custodian. This is in some respects the biggest risk factor of all, as the custodian will lose the lucrative fee income from the investor and will also lose opportunities to do other kinds of business with the investor.

CONCLUSION

This chapter gave detailed information about the nature of the services which fall under the global custody remit. I made the point that although there is doubtless some commoditization in the industry, generally there is still scope for individual custodians to demonstrate to clients that they can inject a considerable edge into their provision of key services.

I categorized global custody services into those which constitute the 'core' of the service and those which amount to 'value added' services which provide scope for custodians to win an edge from the quality of their service provision.

WINNING AN EDGE FROM USING GLOBAL CUSTODY SERVICES

4

INTRODUCTION

Let us again strike what might be termed our conceptual key-note before resuming our theme.

This key-note is the central argument that lies not only at the heart of this book but also constitutes the prime reason for writing it: that global custodians can provide investors with a significant level of competitive advantage. As I emphasized in the Introduction, this competitive advantage is all the more important in an investment world where the widespread access to information about investments means that it is increasingly difficult for an individual investor to gain a consistent performance edge over rivals.

It follows from this that the better the global custody service generally, and the revenue-gathering aspects of the service in particular, the greater the competitive edge that the investor will have a chance of enjoying.

The question of what exactly leading investors think of the role of global custody in their bid for competitive success is of such enormous importance that I approached two of my most prized contacts from the world of fund management and asked them for their comments on this matter. I was interested not only in their perspective on the importance to them of the effectiveness of their

73

global custody services, but also in what they thought of the viewpoint that global custody is something which an investor should do itself.

ROGER FISHWICK

Roger Fishwick is a director of Prudential Portfolio Managers (PPM) and heads the back office team. PPM is the largest institutional investor in the UK, with £115 billion under management as of 30 September 1997. It has eight offices around the world.

Earlier in this book I quoted Roger as being certain that global custodians can offer institutional investors a significant level of competitive advantage and that not enough investors are aware exactly of what custodians can do in this respect. I now look at his views here in greater detail.

'At PPM, we tend to review our commitment to our custodians every three to five years. On the one hand we recognize the great importance of continuity of service; on the other hand we acknowledge that it is necessary to review our custodians so as to ensure that we are obtaining maximum quality of service at all times. This is not to say that we are in any way dissatisfied with our current custodians.

We make our decision about which custodians to use and stick with them according to a wide variety of criteria. Cost is certainly one issue, but it isn't a huge one because we have to look at the level of service provided in its entirety rather than focusing solely on the issue of how much that service costs us.

I would say, in general, that our overall objective in using custody services is to seek to export the risk of holding investments, especially foreign investments. What I mean by this is that we want to have someone else take on the responsibility of the risk which any investment entails from an administrative point of view. I don't mean the risk that the investment will fall or rise, but such factors as the risk that income will not be received *from the investment in time, or that details of any corporate actions won't be forwarded to us.*

Another big risk factor is that of sub-custodian failure. We are always particularly concerned about the danger of this in relation to cash holdings. The reason is that under trust law – which applies in many countries, and especially in the UK and US – stocks are not regarded as belonging to the global custodian or sub-custodian but as owned by the investor. Consequently, the custodian will have to keep stocks in a separate account which is held in trust for the investor. However, cash is not regarded as belonging to the investor in the same way because cash is not 'fungible'; a term which means that it isn't possible to distinguish one cash holding from another. As a result, if a sub-custodian collapsed, we could lose any cash we had deposited with them unless we had some kind of indemnity agreement in place with the global custodian who was making use of that sub-custodian.

In practice, we always insist that our global custodians accept liability for the failure of any sub-custodian they may use, and also that we are provided with indemnities for any failure on the part of our custodians to give us information by the correct date to allow us to take up any benefit due from corporate actions. After all, we ourselves are acting on behalf of other people: we are looking after their money and it is therefore necessary that we act vigorously to maximize their return from their investments.

Similarly, we expect our custodians to be responsible for ensuring that trades are settled in a timely fashion. We would expect them to make up any shortfall deriving from a settlement failure. We also expect them to reclaim tax for us within certain stipulated time limits and, if they cannot do this, to make up the difference to us. I'm not going to tell you how much we spend on our custodians every year in fees, but I can say that we are talking about multiples of million pounds and so we expect a superb service featuring all relevant indemnities. We naturally presume that our custodians will already have in place fidelity insurance – that is, insurance to cover fraud or malpractice by their staff – and that they will also be properly protected against computer fraud of all kinds.'

I went on to ask Roger whether he believed that an institutional investor should handle its own global custody. His reply was an emphatic negative.

'If we at PPM don't handle our own custody, and we're number one in the UK in terms of volume of assets under management, it's obvious we don't think custody is a core skill with which we should be getting involved.'

I also asked him whether he had any other advice for investors about how they should maximize the effectiveness of their relationships with custodians.

'My basic advice is to make sure that the contract you sign with your custodian gives you the level of indemnity you want against failure to deliver the service you need. The contract should also contain detailed and specific clauses about when income should reach you so that you end up with the certain knowledge that funds are coming to you on a certain day. The beauty of being in this situation is that if you can be certain that funds are indeed coming in on a certain date you can to a large extent be fully invested in money-making securities. If you don't have this knowledge you will need to keep a substantial part of your assets in cash so that you can always be sure of being able to discharge regular liabilities when they arise.

I would also say that you need to look hard at the quality of your interface between your organization and your custodian or custodians. Ideally this interface should be entirely electronic; you ought to be able to remove the manual element from the interface completely and with it the inevitable potential for human error which manual interfaces always bring with them. You need to make sure that information can flow easily and accurately between yourselves and your custodian and vice versa.

At PPM we don't start working with a custodian until we have taken them through a detailed process of how we want their system to work and how we want it to interface with our own system. Our custodians have told us they find this induction very helpful as it makes clear to them what we expect of them in both a technological and performance sense. In my view more institutional investors should do this. I feel custodians sometimes perform less well than the investor wants them to perform because the investor simply hasn't made clear how the custodian's systems should interface with the investors and overall what calibre of service is required.

I have no doubt that in the future the emphasis in custody is going to be on straight-through processing, with information flowing in this way between custodian's and investors with no human interference at all unless absolutely necessary.

But just because I do place an emphasis on technology doesn't mean that I have forgotten about the importance of the personal element in the custody/investor relationship. Custodians must hire people who really are in tune with what institutional investors need. They should ideally be career custodians, rather than staff from the banks' retail department who fancy a change. Unfortunately, in the UK custody scene, global custody skills are not rated as highly as they ought to be and consequently the level of professionalism is also not as high as one would like. The situation is completely different in the US, where custody is a highly regarded profession. Not surprisingly, given this attitude, US custodians sometimes come across as being more professional than those in the UK, but not always.'

TONY SOLWAY

Tony Solway is managing director of Henderson Investment Services. Henderson Investment Services is part of the UK fund management group Henderson Investors, which has around £14 billion under management.

Tony is an enthusiastic believer in the notion that an institutional investor should stick to what it is best at and not attempt to handle its own custody. His views are given below.

'There can be no doubt that a custodian can make a big difference to the success of an investment management operation. The most important area of value is the spread of geographical and financial markets catered for by a custodian.

The point is that in an increasingly competitive business world; a world, furthermore, which modern communications and transport are causing to shrink, investors are increasingly sourcing assets at a global level. In other words, an investment management house which wants to succeed long term can't simply confine itself to its domestic markets; it has got to find funds to manage from sources around the world. This was very much our thinking when we opened an office in Singapore recently.

If investments are being sourced from around the world, it is likely that the institutional investor is also going to have to make investments in financial markets around the world to keep its domestic and foreign customers happy. Furthermore, as assets are generally less expensive in emerging markets, most institutional investors will want to invest at least part of their portfolios in these emerging markets.

These different points all lead to one conclusion: an international investment manager needs a global custodian which can really offer worldwide coverage. The institutional investor knows that coverage in emerging markets is going to cost more than similar coverage in developed markets but this is, generally, a price investors are prepared to pay for being looked after in these emerging markets, where investments can be risky but rewards very substantial.'

Like Roger Fishwick, Tony Solway places great emphasis on the role custodians should play in helping investors to manage their risks. Again, he emphasizes that the risks he is talking about relate to the administration of their investments rather than the performance of funds under management.

'Around the world, the general trend is that administrative risks of investing are reducing as developed and emerging markets continue to improve their securities market infrastructure and particularly their settlement and safekeeping systems. However, some serious problems still remain, especially in emerging markets, and we have found that effective local custody activity undertaken by a local custodian bank, with a real in-depth knowledge of how to navigate through what may be extremely complex local conditions, can make a huge difference to the success of investments held in that market. Good custody activity can add value to the investment process all the way down the line, and the more difficult the local market conditions the more true this becomes. We would certainly not consider going into an emerging market without having a first-rate custodian alongside.'

Having canvassed these useful general insights from two fund managers with extensive experience of working with global custodians, I can start focusing the discussion more precisely on what an investor needs to do to head for a situation where it is winning an edge from using global custody services. However, it is unrealistic to assume that most readers of this book will necessarily be in a situation where they can start looking for a global custodian from scratch. Instead, many already have a global custodian in place, either because they have already chosen one or because they inherited one. They may, indeed, have relationships with many custodians.

Consequently, before looking at the process of selecting a global custodian, it is first necessary to examine the usual nature of the relationships between an investor and a custodian.

The most basic relationship between an investor and a custodian occurs when a private investor has a substantial portfolio under management and is personally managing this amount. As can be imagined, some wealthy individuals enjoy taking an interest in the investment of their money and may even take this matter extremely seriously and devote a great deal of time to it. The amount of funds they have under management would have to be high – at least £250,000 or so – to justify the cost of them using the custodian directly, as the custodian's fees would otherwise not be economic.

An institutional investor, on the other hand, pools the investments of many individuals in order to offer the individuals the benefits which always accrue to large investment funds rather than small ones. There is also the important factor that the institutional investor can help individuals by spreading transaction costs and administration costs (which will of course include custody costs) over all the individuals concerned, which will make a great deal of economic sense. In this case, the institutional investor will appoint its own custodian or custodians. The individual investors will not have the financial muscle to influence the decision.

Examples of institutional investors who work with custodians in this way are insurance companies and life assurance organizations, both of which have many private investors who are not actively involved with their investments. Another type of institutional investor which falls into this category would be a pension fund which handles its own fund management in-house.

Things start to become more complicated when we look at specialized investment management companies that have clients who are themselves either large influential private investors or organized investment funds of some kind. Such funds might include pension funds, investment trusts and corporate funds. It is fairly likely that the specialized investment management organization will have been chosen as a result of several such organizations attending what is known within the industry as a 'beauty parade': that is, an opportunity for the investment management organization to present its credentials and, in effect, audition for the privilege of handling the fund. In such cases the relationship between the investment management organization and the fund is very much one of service provider and client, and the last thing the investment management organization wants to do is to alienate or otherwise irritate the client.

Here, the specialist investment management organization will typically inherit a custodian from its client. Some investment management organizations have the commercial power and confidence to request that the client use a custodian with which the investment management organization already has a relationship, but in most cases the organization must abide by the client's choice of custodian. The result of this, is that specialized investment management organizations often find themselves working with a large number of global custodians, not quite a different one for *every* client, because there are not a vast number of global custodians in the world, but very possibly with up to around ten or twelve global custodians. The administrative complications here can often be a serious challenge for investment management organizations, many of whom have no doubt been relieved by the shake-outs and mergers within the global custody industry in recent years.

Once the structure of the relationship between the investor and the custodian has been arranged, the rest is down to the quality of service which the custodian is able to provide, its adherence to the agreed service contract, and the calibre of the people who are working for the custodian. A large part of the burden for making the relationship between the investor and the custodian work falls on the shoulders of the custodian, but the investor must also play its part: ensuring that custodians know what they should be doing and have the right interfaces in place, co-operating with the custodian over such collaborative matters as rights issues, scrip issues and voting, and generally seeking to make the relationship between the investor and the custodian a success rather than giving the custodian the impression that it is continually being auditioned for quality of performance, even after it has received the business.

It is now necessary to look at a question I have already raised: whether the investor needs to use a separate, external custodian at all.

THE DECISION WHETHER OR NOT TO USE AN EXTERNAL CUSTODIAN

The decision as to whether an investor should use an external custodian at all – that is, whether the investor should outsource the custody function – is also a decision about who will carry out the custody function if no external custodian is hired.

For most private investors and pension funds or corporate funds which are not run by investment professionals, the question of handling one's own custody simply does not arise: someone else is going to have to do it. That someone else might be a custodian or perhaps it could be the specialized investment management organization that is handling the management of the assets.

On the other hand, an institutional investor might decide that it will handle its own custody requirements.

To some extent cultural factors play a role in what the final decision is likely to be. In the US, there is a strong culture within the financial industry which accepts that fund management and custody should be different functions. This attitude is reinforced by legislation which actually makes it illegal for a US pension fund to handle its own custody, and generally discourages fund managers from acting as their own custodians in any capacity, and whatever the nature of the fund. In the UK, too, there is a clear trend for institutional investors to use external custodians, although this is not yet enshrined in legislation.

The situation in Continental Europe is very different, however. There, it is quite common for investment managers and other institutional investors to handle their own custody requirements, especially domestic custody. Many also handle their global custody requirements, although there are some which will prefer to farm this out.

In general, I tend to believe that the whole idea of an investment management organisation or institutional investor handling its own custody is a bad one and one that should be phased out throughout the world's financial markets as soon as is feasible.

Why do I think this? Because however much an investment manager or institutional investor succeeds in persuading itself (and, possibly, also its clients) that it is a capable custodian, it is difficult to see that this can possibly be the case. The fact is that investment managers specialize in handling investments and making them grow and/or generate income. Similarly, institutional investors handle investment and also work to market their services and products. These are their core functions; custody, very simply, is not one of them.

True, investors who like to handle their own custody argue that they will have an intimate knowledge of the asset portfolio under consideration, that they will know what global custody services will be required, and – above all – can offer a service that is cheaper than using a global custodian.

Well, it is at least possible that all these may be true. On balance, however, none of them probably will. Specialized global custodians can offer a level of expertise in carrying out this function that investment managers cannot realistically expect to match. Even on the matter of theoretical savings on the cost of hiring a global custodian, it is extremely debatable whether this saving in the fees of the global custodian is a real saving or a false economy. We have already seen that a skilled global custodian can not only speed income generated from assets into investors' bank accounts but can also – through such services as securities lending and tax reclamation – actually generate revenue for the investor.

If an investment portfolio had extensive cross-border investments, it is almost inconceivable that the investor could handle the custody implications of those foreign holdings itself. Even if the investor were to act as the lead custodian in this arrangement, it would still need to use sub-custodians around the world, and it is difficult to see how the investor would have much experience and expertise at selecting such organizations, or co-ordinating their activities.

The problem that the investor will have insufficient expertise and experience to do justice to the challenge of acting as its own custodian – even if this is allowed by national investment industry regulations – is far from being the only problem. There is also the possibility of a serious conflict of interest if the investment management organization or institutional investor attempts to handle its own custody. Its investment managers will be aware of markets where the organization has good custody capabilities and those where it does not. It is difficult to see how fund managers can avoid being influenced in their investment decisions by this knowledge.

Such influence would hardly be in the interests of the holder of the portfolio. It is not difficult to imagine a scenario whereby an investor 'decides' to invest in a market because the investor has laboriously put together the custody capability for that market rather than because the market looks inherently good, or it may also decide not to invest in a market, because they have no custody capability, even though the investment looks promising.

In any event, investment management organizations and institutional investors which attempt to handle their customers custody requirements do not do this for nothing, although it is true they may sometimes not identify the custody service on the invoices. But someone has to pay eventually, and that someone is pretty certain to be the holder of the portfolio, the client, who will ultimately, in effect, be paying for a global custody service which is being administered by people who are not true custody specialists.

On the other hand, the advantages of outsourcing the custody function to a competent specialized domestic or global custodian seem clear. These advantages can be analyzed under three categories:

- risk advantages
- administrative advantages
- cost advantages.

I now look at each of these in turn.

Risk advantages

Security of assets

A specialized global custodian with the very highest level of credit rating is likely to be as close to being a secure haven for investments as it is possible to be. Furthermore, national regulatory structures in all developed countries and many emerging market countries require that custodians keep client assets in separate nominee accounts. Even if the custodian were to fail financially, these nominee accounts are not part of the custodian's resources and would be safe.

Good accounting procedure

While no custodian can completely remove the risk of fraudulent activity relating to a fund, the good accounting procedures used as a matter of course by specialized global custodians will help to safeguard the funds, especially in terms of the assets being held by the global custodian in separate holding accounts that are easily identifiable by the client. If an investment management organization were providing the global custody service, it would probably not be able to offer a similar level of segregation on its books and records.

Freedom from conflicts of interest

A specialized custodian will not have any of the inherent conflicts of interest that can all too easily arise when the investment manager is also responsible for custody.

Compliance officer in place

The specialized global custodian will have a compliance officer, or more likely a compliance team, who will be responsible for ensuring that all the agreed procedures are implemented and adhered to across the board.

Knowledge of major economic and financial indicators

One important advantage of using a specialized global custodian is that it will know (or, at least, should know) about events and developments which could have an adverse effect upon the fund. It will also have an ethical, contractual and (probably) legal obligation to inform the beneficiaries of the fund (or, in the case of a pension fund, the trustees) of these developments.

This is not the same thing as providing investment management advice (which it is not the business of a custodian to provide). It is, on the other hand, very much the business of the custodian to provide factual information on major economic and financial changes which affect the investments. It is generally much easier for a specialized custodian, with its own overseas offices or good network of overseas sub-custodians, to know about important custody-related events on which action must be taken. This is simply a result of the breadth and extent of its information sources dedicated to the provision of custody information.

The 'comfort factor'

There is also the sheer psychological comfort that the investor can enjoy when the custody aspects of the fund are placed with a specialized global custodian. The investor has removed from its own shoulders much of the burden of anxiety which it would have to accept if it acted as its own global custodian. Furthermore, the custodian will almost certainly be obliged to operate within a stringent regulatory framework if it wants to stay in business, and this regulatory framework will usually offer the investor considerable protection, including receiving full value of a holding from a central industry fund should the funds be stolen or otherwise misappropriated by the custodian.

Regulation of the custody industry is in many countries effectively automatic, as the national banking industry is carefully regulated and most global custodians are therefore regulated as banks. Some countries – such as the UK – have separate regulations specifically for the custody industry, but countries with this 'additional' regulatory framework are in the minority.

Administrative advantages

Better quality of information available

A specialized global custodian is constantly taking in and processing high volumes of information relating to crucial matters such as corporate actions and dividend payments. It is unlikely that the custodian – with its extensive range of information and services – would miss a particular action that related to one or more of the assets held by the investor. However, an investor who was trying to handle the custody requirements of a global portfolio without the assistance of a global custodian would be likely to miss many corporate actions.

Better booking

The wider perspective of the specialized global custodian also makes booking more efficient, and results in more comprehensive books which are more useful to the investor. For example, if the investor uses more than one investment management organization, the investor can receive consolidated books across all the managers, rather than having to amalgamate this data in-house.

Faster and higher quality communications

Effective communications between the custodian and the investor are an essential part of the custody service. In general, a specialized global custodian will be able to offer faster and better communications than could otherwise be offered. The reasons for this are that custody is its core, specialized business, not merely an 'add-on' to an investment service, and that its communications technology is likely to be highly efficient.

Access to the specialized global custodian's global network of custody expertise

The chance of the investor, working alone, being able to do justice to the administrative challenges which foreign asset holdings involve, varies from the small to the non-existent. On the other hand, a specialized global custodian has (or should have) access to a global network of custody expertise which it can deploy immediately on behalf of the fund. Another important point in this context is that when an investor uses a custodian which has its own network of offices, or its own disciplined array of sub-custodians, the investor knows exactly with whom it is dealing. This will probably not be the case where the investor uses the custody services of one or more investment managers, all of whom may have different sub-custodian arrangements. The risk resulting from these diversified arrangements will therefore be much greater, as each organization will have different procedures and may also accept differing degrees of responsibility for its network.

Access to proxy voting services

Many investors underestimate the importance of the need for the fund to vote on important matters relating to the corporations in whose securities it has an interest. Keeping track of voting opportunities is difficult enough in the domestic market; where these opportunities arise abroad it may be close to impossible. A specialized global custodian, however, can provide a comprehensive, cross-border service which ensures that no voting opportunity is missed. Proxy voting forms can be provided in good time, and if necessary, a member of staff of the custodian, or of a reliable and trusted sub-custodian, can even attend a meeting in person.

Cost advantages

Better financial returns from the SMAC service

The international experience and the breadth of expertise which the specialized global custodian offers should make for better long-term returns to the trustees on the Securities Movement and Clearance (SMAC) services (i.e. safekeeping and registrations, clearance and settlement, income collecting, corporate action processing).

Better financial returns from the 'value-added' custody service

I have already stated that what constitutes 'value-added' services must to some extent be a matter of opinion. However, one way of looking at value-added services would be to define them as those additional services (i.e. additional to SMAC) which can have a particularly strong impact on the investor's balance sheet and/or competitive profile.

This ability to provide value-added services is a crucial factor – in many ways often the decisive factor – in demonstrating the advantages of the specialized global custodian over any other method of handling the administrative aspects of an investor's investments. No investment management organization can hope to compete with a large, independent global custodian in terms of providing these value-added services which, if managed by an experienced and resourceful custodian, can give the investor considerable benefits, both in terms of reduced administrative costs and enhanced portfolio returns.

Four of the most relevant value-added services from the viewpoint of services that can make money for the investor are as follows:

● securities lending: this gives the investor the opportunity to generate income on securities that would otherwise remain in the custodian's vault;

- cash management: the custodian can actively invest surplus cash balances on behalf of the fund, thereby minimizing income generated from these;
- investment accounting and booking: funds can achieve administrative and cost savings by asking the custodian to provide investment accounting data and consolidated booking across their fund managers;
- performance measurement: analysis of the fund's investment managers' performance against agreed benchmarks is an important benefit which custodians increasingly provide to their customers; this can greatly help to boost an investment manager's ratio of service and overall competitive profile.

With these cost advantages in mind, it is necessary to conclude that ultimately, the cost of using an efficient, specialized global custodian matters less than the cost of *not* doing so.

It follows from the previous discussion that most investors are coming to accept that, when it comes to custody, 'doing it yourself' is unlikely to work. Consequently, selecting a global custodian is one of the most momentous and important decisions an investor can make. The decision both requires an input from, and has repercussions for all areas of the investor's activity. For reasons already explored, the decision is also likely to play a major role in determining the success which the investor enjoys in the future.

SELECTION OPTIONS FACING AN INVESTOR

An investor can select a global custodian in one of the following three ways.

The advantages and disadvantages of each option are also discussed.

Option 1

It can select a global custodian by itself.

Option 2

It can use the services of a consultancy, which will either select the custodian on the investor's behalf, or provide the investor with detailed recommendations. A few large actuarial firms offer consultancy services to investors regarding the selection of custodians. In the UK, for example, such firms include Bacon & Woodrow, Sedgwick Noble Lowndes and the Willis Corroon Group, all based in London, and Watson Wyatt Worldwide, based in Reigate, Surrey. One London management consultancy firm, Thomas Murray, specializes in the global securities services market and is generally regarded as a leading provider of advice on global custodians.

Option 3

It can avoid the responsibility of selecting a global custodian itself by agreeing to use whatever custodian or custody service its investment management organisation (if it has one) is using. Note that if the investor is using several investment management organizations, this could involve the investor in using all the custodians that have a relationship with each respective investment management organisation.

Option 1
The investor selects the custodian itself

Advantages
- The investor retains complete control of the selection process.

- During the selection process, the investor will get to know about the activities of a wide range of custodians and will be able to familiarize itself with the types of services and service levels that can be expected within the industry.

Disadvantages
- The investor may not have the expertise to select the most appropriate custodian for its requirements.
- The investor will have to devote time to the selection process.
- Once it becomes known in the marketplace (as it inevitably will) that the investor is looking for a custodian, the investor is likely to be bombarded by a surprising variety and intensity of sales approaches. Dealing with these can be very time-consuming.
- Sensing the difficulty of the task and aware of their own time constraints, the board of directors (or trustees) of the investor may be tempted to delegate the selection task to a member of staff who is not really qualified to undertake it. While researching this book, I heard of a large institutional investor which had selected a custodian by hiring one of the trustee's daughters (a sixth-form student) during a summer holiday and delegating the task to her. She contacted a number of leading custodians and requested their sales literature. Once she had got all the literature together, she read through it carefully and made the decision. Whether or not her decision turns out in the long-term to have been good or bad for the investor, it must emphatically be pointed out that merely surveying custodians' marketing literature is in no sense an appropriate way to select a custodian.
- It is perfectly possible that when the daunting nature of the task comes home to the investor, the investor will give up trying to make the selection itself and will opt to use a consultancy after all, with the consequent waste of all or most of the time devoted to the task so far.

Option 2
The investor uses a consultancy to select a custodian

Advantages

- The consultancy will remove most of the time burden of the selection process from the investor.
- The investor will gain access to a detailed and comprehensive knowledge of custodian expertise, without needing to be directly involved in the selection process.
- Before starting the selection process, the consultancy will give the investor a detailed questionnaire which, when completed (probably with the consultancy's assistance), will amount to a detailed briefing for the consultancy on the type of custodian the investor is seeking.
- The consultancy's staff will be experienced specialists in the matching of investors to custodians and should be able to draw on a wide breadth of expertise and knowledge of the different skills offered by many different custodians.
- Other things being equal, the consultancy should be able to make better recommendations than the investor could make unaided.

Disadvantages

- The consultancy itself will need to be selected. There are fewer consultancies offering a global custody selection service than there are global custodians, but even so the process of selecting the consultancy will not necessarily be straight-forward.

  In practice, consultancies are usually selected by someone on the board of directors or trustees of the investor having heard of a consultancy and that consultancy being approached. Some consultancies which advise on the selection of global custodians also advise on the selection of investment management organizations, and it may be that the investor will have heard of the consultancy in this manner.

However, the guiding rule of business that it is better to obtain a few quotations before making a selection decision applies as much to the selection of a consultancy as it does to any other area of commercial activity. Investors are well advised to approach a minimum of three consultancies, and obtain their terms of business and details of services. As far as selecting a shortlist of consultancies to approach is concerned, other investors are often more than happy to make suggestions.

- As is usually the case when using a consultancy, the client loses some control over the process which the consultancy is carrying out.

- The investor is obliged to trust to the consultancy's impartiality and objectivity, which ultimately means trusting the consultancy's assurances in this respect. While consultancies usually run to high standards of professional ethics and would not compromise their impartiality in any overt sense, there is no denying that some may have an inherent preference for certain custodians over others, and may therefore be less objective than they may appear.

- Using the consultancy will be relatively expensive. The consultancy will usually charge on a time basis. Daily rates vary, but are likely to be in the vicinity of £1,500. It would be quite routine for a selection process to cost the investor at least £20,000 in consulting fees, and possibly as much as £50,000. For a large investor with a substantial investment portfolio and new funds becoming available for investment every day, spending this amount of money may seem reasonable if the right custodian is chosen. However, in today's highly competitive investment business, these will inevitably make a dent – albeit a temporary one – in the investor's overall financial results.

If the investor wants to use the services of a consultancy to assist with the selection process but has limited funds available for this, the investor could ask consultancies if they were prepared to supply strictly specified information about custodians on an ad hoc basis. It should be possible for the investor to negotiate a price for the supply of this information that is considerably lower – perhaps only a few thousand pounds in total – than the full-scale fee which the consultancy would charge.

The management consultancy Thomas Murray – while it does offer a full-scale consultancy service – is a firm believer in the need for a consultancy to supply highly detailed and structured information if required, and has an extensive database of such information. This information is available for transmission to the client over a data communications system, on disk or on paper.

Finally – as always when using the services of a third-party supplier – the client must agree the precise level of fees in advance, whether the consultancy is supplying a full service or an ad hoc service. Under no circumstances must a consultancy be given the opportunity to rack up additional days of consultants' time beyond what has been agreed in advance. The investor should insist that no more time than was originally foreseen should be devoted to the project, unless it has agreed to this in writing.

Option 3
The investor uses the investment management organization's custodian

Advantages
- As with the decision to use a consultancy, allowing the investor's investment management organization or organizations to appoint their own custodian or custodians will remove most of the time burden of the selection process from the investor's shoulders.

- If the custodian is part of the investment management organization's own corporate group or operating in the same office as the investment management organization there may be more rapid transmission of foreign income collected and better communications generally between the investment management organisation and the custodian.

Disadvantages

- If the investment management organization is trying to handle the custodian duties itself, there are definite potential disadvantages. Most of these stem from the simple fact that few investment management organizations can provide a custody service rivalling that of a custodian which dedicates itself to this service and specializes in it. (*See* Chapter 3 for a fuller discussion of the disadvantages of an investment management organization or an institutional investor trying to handle its own custody.)

- If the investment management organization is using a custodian that is part of its own corporate group, there may be the potential for conflicts of interest that are not to the investor's benefit. However, this problem can usually to a large extent be circumvented by the investor requiring separate agreements with the investment management organization and the custodian over standards and quality of service (these agreements are usually known as service level agreements).

- The investment management organization may be surprisingly possessive of its custodian relationship and may be resentful if the investor tries to break this relationship by suggesting (as the investor has every right to do) that another custodian be used.

On the whole, the reasons investment management organizations usually give for preserving the custodian ties which the organization already has in place – ties that are sometimes presented as sacrosanct rather than as embodying mere commercial expediency – are unconvincing. Business relationships between an investment management organization and a custodian with whom it has worked for a long period are essentially designed to benefit the investment management organization and the custodian rather than the investor. It would be unwise to be too cynical about these relationships – they may result in a high standard of service – but there is nothing inherent about the relationship which will mean that this is necessarily the case.

- If the investor insists on using a custodian of its own choice rather than going along with the investment management organization's request that it be allowed to handle custody as well as investment management, the investment management organization may not be as ready to reduce its fees to accommodate this change as logic suggests.

Few investment management organizations will risk losing a potential new client over the matter of which organization is acting as the custodian. However, if the investor imagines that the investment management organization will reduce its fees if it is no longer also acting as the custodian, it may be surprised to encounter considerable resistance. Some investment management organizations may even suggest that by handling custody as well as investment management, they can derive additional revenue from the custody function – in terms of commissions on foreign exchange transactions and so on – and that this revenue to some extent subsidizes their investment management activity. They might go so far as to say that if they are being deprived of the custodial role their fees for merely providing investment management services should increase. It is not exactly clear whether an investor should respond to this argument by admiring its extraordinary and devious ingenuity or by treating it with something resembling contempt. On balance the latter response seems more appropriate.

As the provision of practical advice is the primary objective of this book, it is essential that some specific advice is given on the precise approach an investor ought to adopt when selecting a custodian. Here, I would make the following recommendations.

- Unless the investor has ample time to make a detailed investigation of at least six global custodians, it ought to consider seeking the assistance of a consultancy.
- If the assistance of a consultancy is sought, the investor should opt for a full consultancy service only if it can readily afford not only the cost of this but also the dent this cost will make in its profits. If the cost is prohibitive, the investor should consider using the consultancy to supply detailed information which the investor can then use to make the selection decision.
- Other things being equal, the investor should avoid using the in-house (as opposed to external) custodian services which it may be offered by one or more of its investment management organizations.
- The investor should only consider using the custodian services of a custodian that has a corporate relationship with the investment management organization but is nonetheless a separate organization both in terms of corporate infrastructure and, probably, location, if separate service agreements can be drawn up with the investment management organization and the custodian.
- The investor should ensure that it keeps in touch with news of the custody industry, so that it can keep abreast of major trends within the industry, particularly including developments at custodians and sub-custodians, and changes and additions to the range of services which custodians offer.
- In the final analysis, and whether or not a consultancy is being used to provide a full service or an ad hoc service, *the investor must remain in control of the selection process*. The decision over

which custodian to use is too important to be delegated away entirely to any external organization. Therefore, even where a consultancy is being used to provide a full service, the consultancy should *not* be required to announce, in effect: 'Your custodian is XYZ Bank.' Instead, the consultancy should be required to announce: 'We believe that you should choose your custodians from the following two or three custodian banks. We are supplying detailed information and recommendations on each one to allow you to make your choice.'

If an investor is to retain control of the selection process, it must understand the principal ways in which custodians differ. The investor should then decide on the principal attributes of the custodian it wants to select. This way, the investor will take control of the selection process from the outset. Rather than present itself to prospective custodians, or consultancies, as a complete beginner as far as selection is concerned, it will present itself as already having a detailed knowledge of the industry and its own requirements within it. This can only help to make the investor selection process more effective, and minimize the likelihood of the investor winding up with an inappropriate custodian.

HOW CUSTODIANS DIFFERENTIATE THEIR SERVICES

If global custodians are right in claiming that their services should not be viewed by investors as mere commodities, it makes sense for investors to expect individual custodians to make an effort to demonstrate an edge in terms of the services they offer, even if the services nominally carry the same description.

In practice, the principal areas in which custodians seek to differentiate themselves are as follows. I have listed the areas in the order of what I perceive to be their importance, with the most important listed first.

- The custodian's credit rating.
- The custodian's capitalisation and general financial credibility.
- The effectiveness of the custodian's SMAC (core) services.
- The effectiveness of the custodian's value-added services.
- The enthusiasm and skills of the custodian's staff. There is a growing consensus within the global custody industry that personal factors are more important than they have ever been when determining how likely the investor/custodian relationship is to be successful. Despite the enormous importance of technology in this relationship, there is no substitute for the personal touch. According to Curt Kohlberg, president of Kohlberg & Associates – a leading US consultancy involved in helping investors select custodians:

'Personal factors matter enormously when a custodian is working for an investor. During the selection process, the investor should take care to meet with the actual people who are going to be handling its business. The investor shouldn't be prepared only to talk to a high-powered team that is detailed to win new business, and whose members aren't seen again by the investor after the business is gained.'

- The breadth of the hours of the day during which the service is available.
- The custodian's multi-language capability.
- The effectiveness of its sub-custodian network and/or network of proprietary offices. This is a major issue, and of particular importance in emerging markets because of the challenges and difficulties these offer. The level of competitiveness among global custodians in this respect is that some will hire a good sub-custodian in a country, even though the global custodian has its own representative office there, if the global custodian thinks that doing this will give it an edge. Furthermore, some

global custodians actively pursue a policy of engaging two sub-custodians in most or all foreign markets in order to give the sub-custodians the chance to compete with one another and to keep them on their toes.

- The custodian's overall ability to minimize custody risk.
- The overall quality of service and adherence to service level agreements.
- The speed with which the custodian responds to enquiries and queries (especially the speed with which the telephone is answered).
- The quality of sub-custodian indemnities (i.e. the extent to which the global custody will indemnify the investor against loss if the sub-custodian defaults or causes some other loss to the investor). The issue at stake here is not usually the threat of actual loss of all assets held by the sub-custodian, as these should be protected by nominee accounts, but rather the risk of incompetence or oversight on the part of the sub-custodian involving the investor in loss. For example, a sub-custodian's failure to communicate details of a rights issue made by a local organization may mean that the investor does not receive what might be substantial benefits to which the investor is entitled.
- Technological sophistication and ability to deliver services electronically.
- A cohesive and readily identifiable corporate structure.
- The general neatness and good order of the custodian's offices.
- The cost of the custodian's services.
- The quality of press coverage offered.

THE SELECTION PROCESS

The investor certainly needs to be aware of all the differentiating points between custodians and to retain ultimate control of the selection decision, but it will not necessarily want to undertake the actual selection process. It must therefore make decisions about the following matters:

- whether it will undertake the selection process itself or use a consultancy, with the consultancy either providing comprehensive assistance or information on an ad hoc basis;
- precisely which areas of custodian differentiation will be of particular importance to the investors' own selection process. The results of this decision will determine those aspects of a custodian's infrastructure, method of operation and quality of service which the investor ought to investigate with particular thoroughness before deciding which custodian to select.

I should again emphasize that even if the investor is using a consultancy to assist with making the selection, it is in my view essential that the investor asserts its control over the selection process.

The next step in the selection process is for the investor, or its consultancy, to draw up what is known as a request for proposal (usually abbreviated to RFP). This, in effect, is a specification of the investor's needs in relation to the custodian.

The request for proposal (RFP)

The precise contents of the RFP will vary from one investor to another according to the nature of their business and their precise needs in terms of asset administration and handling. It would be unwise for this book to be dogmatic about the contents of a particular investor's RFP, just as it would be unwise for a doctor to be dogmatic about a patient's diagnosis until he or she had actually seen the patient. Even so, I can usefully give some general guidance about the contents of the RFP.

Consultancies and investors regard their RFPs as prime elements in their competitive profile and tend to guard the contents of these with some jealousy. However, the consultancy Thomas Murray – which has achieved a truly enviable reputation for the quality of its thought, insight and its absolute integrity – has kindly supplied me with a structure of a typical RFP document. Thomas Murray has, however, asked me to emphasize that it customizes each RFP specifically to a client's own requirements.

Figure 4.1 provides an overview of the RFP document, while Figure 4.2 provides more detailed information about sections 1 and 2 of the RFP.

Once the RFP has been drawn up, the investor or its consultancy can move on to the specific selection process. This process is summarized in Figure 4.3.

An essential part of the selection process is the formulation of a questionnaire which, in effect, interrogates the custodian on its quality of service. This questionnaire will typically be closely based on the RFP, to ensure that the right questions are asked.

As with the RFP, there is no pro forma questionnaire, as the questions which an investor ought to ask will vary from one investor to the next, depending on their RFP. However, a leading custodian has supplied for guidance a list of the questions it is most usually asked by investors (see Figure 4.3).

During the selection process, the investor should find this book's detailed analysis of the ways in which custodians differentiate themselves – and the percentages attached to these factors – an important aid to an evaluation exercise which can otherwise seem impossibly complex and demanding. By using this information, the investor can ensure that instead of being at the mercy of the custodian's sales team (or the consultancy's advice), it can itself establish and maintain a firm control over the selection process by showing it that knows what it wants, and by being insistent that it intends to get it.

The investor's RFP should be circulated to at least a dozen custodians which the investor or its consultancy has reason to believe are likely to fit the bill as far as its requirements are concerned. Based on an evaluation of responses to these RFPs, the investor should aim to draw up a shortlist of two to five custodians which can be investigated in greater detail.

Figure 4.1 The RFP document

This document is divided into seven main sections, illustrated below.

Section 1	Contains a profile of the buyer and the background to the selection process
Section 2	Covers questions relating to all those matters that are considered by the buyer to be critical to its custodial arrangements. The level of response required in this section should be sufficient to determine whether the candidate can meet the key selection hurdles the buyer has established in the RFP process.
Sections 3–7	Involve broader and deeper investigations of specific items raised in Section 2, including credentials, basic and added value service provision, booking and communications, and fees.

Contents

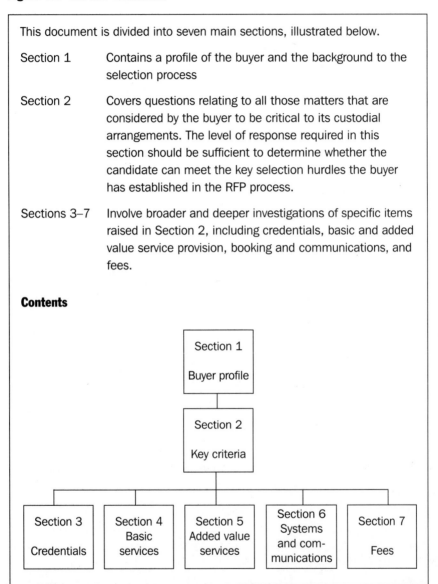

Source: Thomas Murray

Figure 4.2 Areas to be included in an RFP

Section 1: Buyer profile (i.e. investor profile)

This section should provide a brief introduction to buyer's business, its global custody requirements, and key buying criteria (for example, the emphasis placed on different areas of service). It should also include the statistics required by candidates to calculate fees.

- An overview of the buyer's business and structure.
- A description of its client base and product mix.
- Background to the RFP, including objectives and requirements.
- The buyer's key buying criteria and hurdles.
- The scope of business to be included in the RFP.
- Relevant statistics:
  - asset holdings: by product segment, instrument (equities/bonds), and market/country
  - transactions volumes: by product segment, instrument (equities/bonds), and market country
  - lines of stock, number of cash movements and accounts, contracts (for derivatives) etc.

Section 2: Key criteria

This section should cover no more than 30 questions relating to all those matters that are considered by the buyer to be critical in assessing the suitability of a particular candidate. The level of response required in this section should be sufficient to determine whether the candidate can meet the key selection hurdles established by the buyer. The remainder of the RFP examines service areas in more depth. *Every buyer will need critically to determine its own key criteria according to its own particular requirements, based on an understanding of best market practices.*

Examples of key criteria include:

- credit ratings;
- service and systems availability/specifications (in core service areas, and by market)*;
- location and staffing of proposed account team;
- client and asset mix, including key wins and losses;
- materiality of global custody business to the rest of the organisation;
- level of investment in people and systems – now and going forward;
- provision of indemnities and guarantees;
- responsibilities for (specified) risks;

Figure 4.2 continued

> ● attitudes to strategic partnerships.
>
> *For example: does the global custodian offer contractual settlement in all markets where the buyer currently invests?

Source: Thomas Murray

Figure 4.3 The RFP process

> The questions below set out the main steps which a buyer needs to go through in order properly to evaluate its needs and carry out an RFP exercise.
>
> **Organisation and control**
> Briefly describe your organisation, indicating where custody sits within it.
> Please provide a geographical breakdown of custody assets held world-wide. Please also define by type of asset held.
> How do you measure your performance in the market place?
> What are your present credit ratings?
> Does your organisation and network of sub-custodians comply with ERISA I7f5?
> What insurance cover do you have within your custody area?
> Please provide a brief summary of your main strengths
> What future developments are being planned at present in the following areas:
>
> ● IT
> ● service
> ● network.
>
> **Network**
> Please list your sub-custodians by country, detailing those countries where you use your own offices.
> What are the key criteria for selecting a sub-custodian?
> How do you monitor the performance of your sub-custodians? Please provide examples of the service levels you have in place.
> Do you accept liability for losses caused by yourselves and your sub-custodians?

Figure 4.3 continued

Client service

How will you service the client?

- State the number of personnel that will manage the relationship.
- Are they split between front and back office?
- How do you differentiate between each sector (i.e. pension fund/investment manager)?

Describe your query tracking facilities.
How do you keep your client up-to-date with market information?
How will you manage the transition process?

Methods of communication and booking facilities

How will you communicate with the client:

- for receiving instructions
- for sending confirmations
- for providing information
- for providing books.

Please provide examples of books available. Differentiate between hard copy and on-line books.
Please describe the functionality of your booking facilities.

Systems

Briefly describe your computer systems architecture.
Please outline any major systems developments planned for the next two to three years.
What disaster recovery plans are in place for your systems?

Core services

Settlement
- In what markets do you provide Contractual Settlement? Please determine your understanding of this contractual service.
- Please provide your cut-off times for instructions.
- Do you provide a pre-matching facility?
- How do you manage failed trades?

Income
- In what markets do you provide Contractual Income?
- Do you pre-advise your client of income due?
- Do you manage market claims on behalf of the client?

Figure 4.3 continued

Tax reclaims
- In what markets do you provide Contractual Reclaims?
- How do you manage the tax reclaim process?
- Please detail the time taken to reclaim tax in each market.

Corporate actions
- What sources of information do you use for corporate actions?
- How soon do you notify the client of a corporate action after its announcement?
- Please provide your cut-off times for instructions.
- Do you manage market claims on behalf of the client?

Proxy voting
- In what markets to do you provide this service?
- Please provide cut-off times for instructions.
- Is this an active or a passive service?

Securities lending
- In what markets do you provide this service?
- Please describe the lending programmes you have available.

Value-added services

Investment accounting
- Do you have a full multi-currency investment accounting system?
- What are the main features of this system?
- Please provide examples of the types of books available through this system.

Performance measurement
- Do you have an investment management system?
- What are the main features of this system?
- Please provide examples of the types of books available?

Derivatives clearing
- Do you offer a global traded futures/options contract clearing service?
- Is the information integrated into your custody and accounting systems?
- Please provide examples of the types of books available?

Figure 4.3 continued

Safekeeping
- Do you hold securities in omnibus or segregated accounts?

Cash management
- Do you provide interest-bearing current accounts?
- Do you require a minimum balance to be held on accounts?
- What overnight facilities are available to the client?
- Do you provide overdraft facilities?
- Please provide cut-off times for instructions.
- Please list the currencies in which your institution makes a market for the purpose of supporting foreign exchange.
- Please list the current interest rates offered to clients on cash balances.

Source: Morgan Stanley.
Note: Morgan Stanley has now pulled out of the global custody industry but this figure is still highly instructive.

For obvious reasons, the investigation of the potential global custody must focus on the precise ways in which the custodian would handle the investor's requirements on a day-to-day basis. This is a complex and highly detailed investigative process. Even if the investor has not used a consultancy so far, it should consider doing so if it does not have specific experience of carrying out this detailed investigation.

It is particularly important that this final stage of the selection process contains an investigation of the standard of care that the custodian will be able to provide for the investor's assets, in all the countries where the investor holds assets. Figure 4.4 provides what can be considered as a pro forma standard of care, with all the important points included.

Figure 4.4 Standard of care

This section reviews your security processing operations procedures. It provides us with information regarding the standard of care that you will warrant to us in the handling of our customers' assets.

Security receipts and deliveries

Please describe your process for handling receipts and deliveries, and include in your response the following information.

● Are copies of delivery tickets receipted and returned?
● Are certificates examined for good delivery, at what stage of the receipt process are they examined, and what checks are performed?
● Is there a procedure for determining if certificates received have been booked missing?
● Are certificate numbers recorded on receipts and deliveries? How is this effected?
● Are certificates microfilmed? Are both sides of the certificates (and attached coupons) filmed?
● Is a file of uncompleted transactions maintained by the receiving department?
● What is your process for referring/following up on uncompleted transactions/fails? Will you automatically attempt redelivery on sale fail? How often?

Securities transfer

Please describe your operations processing with regard to registering securities into the appropriate names to ensure protection of entitlements. Include in your description the following points.

● Within what time frame are registered securities received in and forwarded to the transfer department and then out for registration?
● Describe the procedures that are in place to ensure all securities are sent for registration.
● How frequently are outstanding transfer items reviewed to determine that transfers are being completed on a timely basis?
● Are certificates examined upon their return from the transfer agents to determine that they have been registered as instructed?
● Describe your procedures for dealing with securities rejected by registrars.
● Are the new certificate numbers recorded?

Figure 4.4 continued

- Describe the procedure for agreeing holdings to the registrar.

Entitlements and income collection

With regard to collection of entitlements on securities held, please describe the process and sources used to gather information on entitlements and to collect and process those entitlements to your customers. Please address the following in your discussion.

- What are your procedures for handling market claims? What booking do you provide and actions do you take to ensure timely collection?
- Are you able to provide 'Relief at Source' from excess withholding tax deductions?
- What is your process for handling tax payments and reclaims resulting from entitlements received?
- What are the expected time lapses in processing tax reclaims and what are the deadlines within which a filing must be made?

Other

- What is the notification process used to identify and handle fraudulent certificates?
- Do you accept liability for ensuring the genuineness of share certificates?
- Is there a separation of duties among those individuals who:
  - initiate transactions
  - maintain books of records
  - receive or disburse funds
  - maintain custody over securities
  - pull and cut coupons?
- Have you identified a contingency plan to ensure continuance of operations and systems in place? When was it last tested? Has it ever been put into effect? Please describe in general terms the plan you have established, the frequency of testing, how it gets implemented and your plans to inform your customers of the requirements under the contingency plan.
- Please provide details of any occasion when such a contingency plan has been relied on, and its efficiency.

Security control

In describing your control procedures, please be sure to cover the following.

Figure 4.4 continued

In addition, please also provide the data requested in the vault section.

● Are identification cards and/or passwords used to secure admission to vault areas? Is there an active log kept of those granted access?
● Is a surveillance system or closed circuit television cameras and video monitors used, and where?
● Is a schedule for inspecting, testing and servicing all security devices maintained?
● Is identification required to be shown before access to the vault is permitted?
● Are persons other than custodian employees required to be escorted to the vault by Bank personnel?
● Is a log book for visitors to the vault maintained?
● Are briefcases, etc. required to be kept outside of the vaults which contain securities?
● Please provide details on the filing process within the vault. Are files maintained by security or by account? Will accounts be segregated through the use of individual deposit boxes or will you utilize a shared space securities vault?
● Is dual control established and maintained for the safekeeping of:
  – assets held in safes and vaults
  – all keys to safes and vaults
  – codes, ciphers and test keys
  – data processing memory storage facilities (tapes, files, disks, etc.)?
● Is dual control established and maintained for the handling of all securities, negotiable and non-negotiable?
● What are your waste paper treatment and disposal procedures?

Data security
Describe your data security measures. Please include the following topics in your discussion.

● Is there a formal filing system for tapes, disks and other data storage devices?
● Are precautions taken to ensure that the information contained on tapes/disks is protected?
● Are back-up programs and tapes/disks stored on or off premises? Please provide a description of protected storage places and classes of safes and record containers used.

Figure 4.4 continued

Record keeping

Please provide an overview of your securities movement control process, your record-keeping process and your booking processes. Include in your discussion a review of your interaction with any depositories in use in your country. Please include in your response the following.

● Are all certificates received in or delivered out of the vault recorded on the date of movement?
● Is a record maintained showing the location of all securities for which you are accountable?
● Can memorandum entries be recorded to show securities owned by the account for which the custodian is not accountable?
● What is the frequency with which securities positions listings and statements can be obtained?
● Is there a formal reconciliation program with the registrars and central depository (if used)? Please provide a description of the reconciliation process.
● How is data entry accuracy assured through input/output devices?
● Is a history system which records all processed transactions maintained? What is the span of time during which information can routinely be retrieved?

Record retention

Please describe your standard record retention process and control. Include in your response the time frames involved and the following.

● Is there a formal procedure for retaining records?
● How are such records stored (microfiche, hard copy, magnetic tape, etc.)?
● Please provide a description of the retrieval system.

Data processing procedures and controls

Please cover the following in addition to an overview of your current and future environment. Be sure to focus on the controls you have in place and/or are implementing (plus the time frame for implementation).

● Is the DP system programmed to detect attempts to access the central unit from an unauthorized terminal or site?

● Is output reconciled by persons who do not prepare the input or handle the process?

Figure 4.4 continued

- Is there a formal contingency plan to deal with disrupted operations?

Internal audit

When discussing the internal audit control process and structure, please be sure to cover the following:

- Is a committee charged with responsibility for supervising the auditor and the auditing department and reviewing and approving the internal audit program?
- Does the audit program focus on securities processing, data programming and financial operations?
- Does the audit program include a review of the operation of the central depository?
- Are all premises, including data processing centres and facilities included in the audit program?
- How frequently are securities counted and agreed to the balances shown on the custodian's accounting records?
- How often are full internal audits made?
- What is the method used to ensure that internal audits are not conducted in a predictable cycle?
- Are written audit books made and to whom?
- Are arrangements and procedures available for customer's internal and external auditors to perform audits on the custodian's premises and can such audits include certificate counts and review of controls and procedures?

External audit

With regard to your external audit program, please include in your discussion the following. Please include in your response to this RFP the most recent letter from the external auditors commenting on the custodian's internal controls.

- What is the name of the outside firm of accountants who performs the audit?
- Does your audit committee review the scope of the auditing procedures of the independent accountants?
- What tests are performed in connection with the accountants examination?
- Does the committee receive books issued by the accountants directly,

Figure 4.4 continued

and meet with them periodically to discuss the results of their work?
● Does the firm of accountants, or equivalent, regularly review the system of internal controls and if so with what frequency?

Regulatory environment and examinations
In discussing the regulatory environment in which you work, please provide the following information.

● What are names of regulatory agencies which conduct unannounced examinations?
● Do agencies book their findings to the custodian's Board of Directors?

Source: The author

MONITORING THE CUSTODIAN'S PERFORMANCE

Replacing a custodian once it has been appointed is far from being an easy, or inexpensive, task for the investor.

It is consequently particularly important that everything possible should be done at the selection stage to ensure that the correct custodian is chosen the first time. However, ongoing monitoring of the custodian's activities and standard of work on the investor's behalf must continue after the custodian has been appointed. In a worst case scenario, if an exemplary level of service is not being delivered, the investor must give the custodian fair warning of ending the relationship if the level of service does not improve.

The ongoing monitoring process should cover every aspect of the working relationship, with particular reference to the following issues.

● Is the custodian providing at every level the standard of service it has contractually agreed to provide?
● Is the standard of care being adhered to?

- Is the level of person-to-person service being provided by telephone and (where appropriate) face-to-face what the investor can reasonably expect?
- Are the custodian's foreign branches performing to expectation?
- Are the lead custodian's sub-custodians performing to expectation?
- Are the custodian's communications facilities (especially the electronic facilities) between the investor and the custodian performing to expectation?
- Is the custodian's overall approach to doing business and level of professionalism what the investor can reasonably expect?

THE CONTRACT BETWEEN THE INVESTOR
AND THE CUSTODIAN

A final, absolutely crucial element in an investor's successful use of global custody services lies in the accurate thoughtful and proper formulation of the contract which the investor signs with its global custodian.

In many cases this contract will be drawn up by the custodian and presented to the investor as something of a *fait accompli*. However, I believe this to be a far from satisfactory way of doing things. In my view, it is ideally the *investor* who should initiate the contract generation process.

The point is that the global custodian is always going to make life easy for itself if possible. The draft contract it provides will not necessarily contain the built-in need to give the investor the very best level of service. Instead, I like the approach outlined earlier in this chapter by Roger Fishwick, in which he said that he insists on certain terms being met by custodians with whom he works. Not all investors will have the financial muscle of Roger Fishwick's organisation, but I think his is the right approach.

Figure 4.5 shows an example of a representative contract between an investor and a custodian. We do not recommend that readers simply adopt this in its entirety, but rather that they use it as the basis for negotiations. It has been provided to me by a major custodian on a strictly unattributable basis.

Figure 4.5 Draft service level agreement

INTRODUCTION

Details of Custody and Settlement Services provided by . . . .
. . . . to . . . . or its appointed agent are shown in this document and should be read in conjunction with Custody and/or other Agreements that may be in existence.

Updates to this document by the Bank will be issued and forwarded to the customer from time to time.

CLIENT AUTHORITIES

Custody and Settlement Services will accept instructions in accordance with the Bank mandate in force.

METHODS OF COMMUNICATION BETWEEN INVESTOR AND CUSTODIAN

(a) Proprietary electronic communications system.
(b) Mail: letters, contract notes, etc. should be sent to the appropriate address as follows:
   UK Securities . . . . Foreign Securities . . . .
(c) Telex: we recommend that all telex instructions should be sent by tested telex using keys provided by the Bank. Our telex numbers are as follows: . . . .
   Prior to using this form of communication for instructions an Indemnity Form (see Appendix 1) should be in our hands.
(d) Fax: all instructions should be addressed as for mail above. Prior to using this form of communication for instructions an Indemnity Form should be in our hands. The appropriate fax number should be in our hands. The appropriate fax number should be used as follows: . . . . . .
   . . . .

Figure 4.5 continued

(e) SWIFT: SWIFT messages and instructions can be accepted in the appropriate format. Our details for SWIFT are as follows: . . . .
. . . .

(f) Telephone: in special circumstances where time is of the essence, telephone instructions will be accepted provided an Indemnity Form (see Appendix 1) is in our possession. A written confirmation of the telephone instruction should be provided within two business days.

It is accepted that either party may electronically record such communication.

SETTLEMENTS

A list showing the countries where we offer the choice between Contractual Settlement Date Accounting (CSDA) and Actual Settlement Date Accounting (ASDA) is available. For Institutional customers we would recommend for Overseas Trades CSDA is taken. It must be borne in mind that in certain countries local market conditions etc. preclude us from providing a full contractual settlement service and for sales it is necessary to use ASDA. There are instances where CSDA will not apply and they are as follows.

(a) If securities are sold in a centre other than where they are physically held.
(b) If securities are sold in non-local currency.
(c) If shares are out for registration and certification cannot take place in time or securities are not generally available in the market.
(d) If receipt of the stock or a delivery has failed for a period in excess of one month after contractual settlement, we reserve the right after consultation with the client to reverse the cash entries with an interest adjustment or back valuation as necessary.

The Bank is an Institutional Net Settlement Participant (NSP) and we would normally expect corporate customers to conduct their relative UK business within the INS system.

For UK equities both INS and non-INS we prefer instructions within 48 hours of dealing but in any event no later than midday on the Trade date plus 2, (T+2) to enable us to process work for all clients in an orderly fashion. We believe our deadline is a reasonable target, but we have retained a time cushion to allow a safety net in which we can usually

Figure 4.5 continued

handle situations where for many different reasons clients deliver instructions late. This operation is, of course, on a 'best endeavours' basis.

Gilt and cash deals should be advised as soon as possible after dealing but in any event no later than 10.00 a.m. on settlement day.

CORPORATE ACTIONS
We would normally expect to advise details of corporate actions on the clients relative holding within three business days of receipt of the documentation from the company or advice from the sub-custodian. Although we do have prior notification of issues in the UK, it is necessary to ensure that our holdings are reconciled with the Registrar and the correct entitlement is received.

For mandatory corporate actions we will implement the appropriate action. For non-rnandatory events we will take action on receipt of the clients instructions by the deadline date notified to the client on each occasion.

For corporate actions of a difficult nature we normally require instructions 48 hours before the closing dates, although we fully understand that there may be a necessity in some circumstances to leave a decision to the last minute. In this event we would ask that the client approaches the corporate action section who will supply a new deadline which would be as close to the company's last date for acceptance as practicable.

If however an instruction is not received by 48 hours before the company's closing date, we would make every effort to contact the client by telephone to obtain instructions unless a default action is shown. All instructions received late will be dealt with on a 'best endeavours' basis and a courier service can be provided at the expense and on the instruction of the client. Under SFA regulations we are prohibited from taking any action if client's instructions are not received.

For proxy voting we will notify clients of all Extraordinary General meetings within three business days of receipt of documentation.

Proxy forms will be completed in accordance with clients' instructions and deadlines will apply in line with Corporate Actions, although it should be borne in mind that the deadline for receipt of postal votes is normally 48 hours before the meeting.

Figure 4.5 continued

Company books will be sent out as soon as possible if specifically requested but a time delay will occur because a re-order will need to be made to the company.

INCOME

Although the Bank does not offer guaranteed value date payments, we do provide a high standard of service in this respect, which we constantly look to improve upon. Income collection facilities are currently available from 35 countries. A chart giving details is available.

Entitlements are calculated on your traded position at ex-date which is the total holding upon which you will receive the dividend, provided the stock has been registered.

Market claims

Where a client is entitled to a dividend but the stock has not been delivered to our agents, or has not been registered, we claim the dividend automatically and credit your bank account upon receipt of the funds.

If we receive a market claim against us we always ask for client permission to settle.

TAX RECLAMATION

A tax reclamation service is available to clients or their nominated agents if required. The details are as follows.

We would look to send tax reclaim forms to you for exhibition to the Revenue within one month of the payment date, although where volumes are low this may be up to two months. Reclaims are forwarded to our sub-custodian or the appropriate fiscal authority immediately on their return by you. Approximate time periods before receipt of the refund in the main countries are listed separately.

We have a PC system which collates all dividends on which reclaims are due and prepares forms etc. If required we can provide a range of books in various formats, e.g. by country, by due date etc.

CURRENCY TRANSACTIONS

When you book Foreign Exchange deals elsewhere please advise your

Figure 4.5 continued

brokers/bankers that they should arrange settlement with our correspondent banker, a list of whom is available.

RECONCILIATIONS

Stock: on receipt of a list of securities we would expect you to advise us of any discrepancies in your portfolio within ten business days of receipt of the list, otherwise the book will be taken as correct.

Cash: we would expect you to notify us of any discrepancies relating to your bank account as soon as possible but no later than ten business days.

Response time: we will send an acknowledgement within two business days of receipt of notice of any discrepancies and would expect to advise you of the results of our investigation of the discrepancies within ten business days of our acknowledgement.

Audit requests: all audit requests will be dispatched within ten business days of the booking date provided standing instructions are in existence or a request is received before the booking date.

Reconciliation of assets: in addition to internal audits, the department carries out its own audit which consists of a six-monthly rolling check of certificates for UK companies and, for Held Abroad securities, a monthly reconciliation with our sub-custodians.

BOOKING

The Bank currently provides two books via our proprietary electronic system: a List of Securities Book detailing contracted positions of holdings, broken down by currency, and a Holdings by Location Book which advises of stock available for delivery.

Information can currently be accessed on-line to our proprietary electronic system between 8.30 a.m. and 5.30 pm Monday to Friday. Phase II will provide an automated upload and download facility during the night at a time slot allocated by the Bank while still allowing on-line access throughout the day.

Apart from communicating via our proprietary electronic system, the Bank communicates by letters requesting instructions for corporate actions,

Figure 4.5 continued

proxies etc. and provides hard copy portfolio valuations plus tax vouchers and paper advices of settlements and other movements.

ENQUIRIES

We endeavour to respond to clients' enquiries as soon as possible but undertake, apart from items of an exceptional nature, usually involving third parties, to resolve all enquiries provided that all the relevant information has been passed to us, within the following time scale.

Time enquiry received from date of transaction	*Time taken to resolve problem after enquiry date of transaction*
Up to 5 business days	Within 2 business days
From 6 business days to 3 months	Within 14 business days
From over 3 months to a year	Within 21 business days
Over one year	Within 30 business days

A list of named contacts is available to whom you should address enquiries. If a satisfactory response is not received within the time scale the matter should be referred to the management team.

SECURITIES LENDING

The Bank agrees to provide administrative facilities to accommodate securities lending as and when required and will act as an agent on behalf of the investor. Stocks and shares will only be lent through money brokers appointed by the investor from time to time and we undertake to observe any limits and other restrictions the investor imposes on collateral or amounts lent to money brokers. Stock lending will not commence until the relative agreement between the investor and its chosen moneybrokers is in place and a copy provided to the Bank.

In acting on behalf of the investor the Bank will be bound by the rules defined in the securities lending agreement which the investor enters into with its chosen money broker and shall be obliged to act in accordance with current market practices, customs and conventions. Any losses suffered by the investor as a result of the Bank observing the aforementioned rules, market practices etc. will not be the responsibility of the Bank except in cases where the cause has been due, in whole or in part, to the negligence and/or failure of performance of the custodian or any of the custodian's appointed agents.

Figure 4.5 continued

While the Bank's computer prograrn will automatically process dividends on stocks and shares which have been lent, the Bank will require to rely on the moneybrokers to account to it for the amounts due. In the unlikely event of a moneybroker failing to make dividend payments, the Bank would look to the investor to make good any loss incurred.

Collateral will be checked for total value and the Bank shall of course exercise the same degree of care in checking items received on behalf of the investor as it would if it were acting on its own account. Interest due from moneybrokers will be checked and claimed by the Bank for credit to the investor's account under advice at the end of each month.

The investor confirms by signing this agreement that it has full authority to participate in stock lending. Details of moneybrokers, limits on collateral and loans, interest rates, fees payable to the Bank and other relative matters will be set out and agreed between the Bank and the investor.

MISCELLANEOUS MATTERS

Insurance. We have in place fidelity and professional indemnity insurance for an amount of *not less than £50 million*.

Designation. It is possible to have a designation added to the name of the nominee company for UK holdings and this service may be activated by the customer at any time.

Disaster recovery – system failure

Hardware. The IBM Mainframe is duplicated across a specifically designed dual module arrangement. The VAX is covered by a specialist disaster recovery company in the event of major system failure. Maintenance agreements exist in the event of less serious problems. Implementation of further contingency arrangements are underway for the VAX. This entails clustering of the VAX 6420 with a VAX 6510, to provide a 'hot standby'. Volume shadowing of all disks has been introduced. The Bank's disaster recovery arrangement for the VAX hardware is tested on at least an annual basis.

Software. The software is covered by a four hour response maintenance agreement with the supplier (A~). In practice the response times have not given cause for concern.

Overseas correspondents. An up-to-date list of our agents is available.

Figure 4.5 continued

APPENDIX I

To: The Custodian Bank

Gentlemen,

We, ... having our Registered Office at . .

. . . .

Considering that from time to time we wish to instruct receipt or delivery of securities against payment to any other person, firm or organisation wheresoever held, *and considering also that* for the sake of convenience we have requested that you will accept instructions to give effect to such transfers notwithstanding that these instructions will be given to you by us by telephone/telex/facsimile and not retrospectively be confirmed to you in writing, to which request you have acceded; *now therefore we do hereby* undertake to indemnify you and hold you harmless from and against all and any claims, losses, consequence of your acting upon instructions received by telephone/telex/facsimile to effect such transfers of securities against payment as set out above, or in connection therewith in any manner or way provided that such claims, damages and expenses do not arise from the negligence and/or failure of performance, whether wholly or partially, of the Bank, its Servants or Agents.

Yours faithfully

. . . . date . . . .

One matter of great importance not covered by Figure 4.5 is the need for the investor and custodian to agree to precise levels of compensation and indemnity to be provided by the custodian in the event of anything going wrong. Something is almost bound to go wrong at some point and so these provisions are extremely important. They will usually be the grounds for hard negotiation between the investor and the custodian. Investors should negotiate hard here, and should remember that if any provision is *not* included, the law will assume that it is not covered. Investors seeking a competitive edge from using a global custodian must pay particular attention to all contractual issues. The job should not all be delegated to the investor's lawyers, because they may not have the detailed level of expertise required to ensure that the investor's interests are properly looked after in the wording of the contract.

However, precise as the terms providing for indemnity and compensation should be, the investor is ill-advised to press so hard for a tough deal that the custodian becomes disenchanted, or is in a situation where handling the investor's business becomes unprofitable. Besides, there are also personal factors to consider. If you are an investor, do you really want to give the custodian, with whom you should be nurturing a co-operative and mutually beneficial relationship, the impression that you are watching it like a hawk and will strike the instant there is the slightest deviation from the level of service specified in the contract? Of course you are entitled to compensation and protection where there has been a serious oversight or other instance of incompetence, and the very fact of clauses covering compensation being in the contract at all will tend to put pressure on a custodian not to deviate from the standard of service required. But investors need to consider that the very people whom they will be accusing of incompetence or of having committed an oversight if they are putting in a claim for compensation, will be the same people with whom they will have to deal the following day on some custody matter. Continual claims for modest amounts of compensation are hardly going to help the success of the investor/custodian relationship. And, above all, despite the proliferation of technology and despite all the technical issues at stake in the custody process, this relationship is what matters and is what is going to determine the success of the whole venture of the investor delegating the custody function to one or more external custodians.

CONCLUSION

This chapter considered how investors can win an edge from using global custody services. I provided details of interviews with Roger Fishwick of Prudential Portfolio Managers, and Tony Solway of Henderson Investment Services. Both these highly experienced professionals accept that global custody can play a key role in helping investors win a competitive edge, especially in terms of how custody helps investors to manage risks.

This chapter also gave information about how an investor should decide whether or not to use an external custodian and focused on the advantages of outsourcing the custody function to a competent global custodian organisation. I categorized these advantages as falling into three areas: risk advantages, administration advantages and cost advantages.

I then went on to look at the various options for how the investor should go about selecting the custodian and what type of selection criterion should be observed.

Finally, I gave information about how the investor should monitor the custodian's performance, and how the contract between the investor and custodian should be drawn up.

THE COST OF USING AN EXTERNAL GLOBAL CUSTODIAN

5

INTRODUCTION

In Chapter 4, I made the question of cost a relatively low priority among the areas where custodians can differentiate themselves from one another. However, this is not to say that the question of the cost of the global custody service is an unimportant matter in absolute terms. In fact, it is a major concern to all investors.

Competition within the fund management industry is extremely fierce, clients being perfectly prepared to switch from one investor to another without hesitation if they believe another will bring better fund performance. Even where a investor is doing its utmost to maximize the performance of funds under management and to deliver to its own customers a first-rate quality of service, its efforts to excel in these respects will be in vain if it is not also paying strict attention to costs.

Custody services are among the most important external services that an investor can buy in. It follows that paying careful attention to costs when making use of custody services is an essential element in an investor's overall cost management activity. By extension, a global custodian that seeks to remain competitive must adopt a competitive attitude towards costs.

But an investor can only make a cost-effective use of custody services if it understands how custodians levy charges, what the market rate for their services generally is, and how the investor can best *make money* from using custody services.

Investors who decide to allow a global custodian to handle their worldwide custody requirements save themselves an additional level of complexity. If the investor were trying to do the job itself it would have to look at cost-effectiveness both from the perspective of dealing with the global custodian and also from that of dealing with the sub-custodian. Today, when most major investors will be liaising with a lead custodian (i.e. a global custodian) who will handle their worldwide custody requirements, the most important aspect of cost-effective use of custody services relates to the use of the global custodian.

MAJOR COST CONSIDERATIONS

Laurie Baker, network manager at Lloyds Bank Securities Services in London, commented:

> 'In my view, global custodians' charges are so important in the custodian selection process that they should be the next criterion investigated after the investor has analyzed whether the prospective custodian is able to deliver what is required in a functional sense. In other words, you first need to make sure that the prospective custodian is going to be able to offer a highly efficient custody service across all the categories of instruments you require and in all the markets, and then you need to make sure they are going to be competitive in what they charge you.'

Laurie Baker said he accepted that the question of global custodians' charges was a complex one and that many investors would need guidance through it; especially if they were engaging a custodian for the first time.

'Broadly speaking, there are two ways in which global custodians charge for their services. Firstly, they may offer what is known as a "bundled fee", which covers all the services which the investor is likely to need during the period to which the fee relates: typically a 12-month period. A global custodian will usually only be willing to quote a bundled fee if it can obtain some fairly detailed information about the type and quantity of business it will be handling on behalf of the investor.

At the very least it will want to know in which markets the investor is investing – including all foreign markets, of course – and what the probable throughput of volume of business is going to be in each market. Obviously, without this information, it will hardly be in a position to put in a realistic quotation for the business. Even after it has obtained this information, it will still attach certain conditions to the quotation. These are basically tolerances which provide for an additional fee to be paid if the investor's activities mean that the custodian has got to be handling more work than was originally provided for when the bundled fee was agreed.'

The second option is for the global custodian to quote a different fee for each of the countries in which the custody service is being provided. Here, the fee charged will be based around what the global custodian will have to pay any sub-custodian it uses in the country in question. As sub-custodian fees vary considerably from one country to the next, and indeed among different sub-custodians in the same country, careful attention to the details of the quotation on the part of the investor is essential.

Useful as it would be to set down here precise information about the level of costs which a investor can expect to pay when using the services of a global custodian, the truth is that matters are not as simple as that. The reason is because, as Laurie Baker explains, 'Each different user of custody services in effect represents a different case, and each case has to be looked at in relation to all the different kinds of services it will require during the time-period in question. It's like asking how much it costs to buy a car; the answer depends entirely on what type of car you want.'

There are, however, certain general points which can be made regarding the cost of using a global custodian. The fundamental point to make is that most custodians operate a two-level charging structure. This is based around:

(a) the market value of the assets being handled by the custodian
(b) the various trade settlements which must be made by the custodian on behalf of the investor.

Generally – although the reader should beware of taking this as an invariable rule – the cost of providing the main global custody services to the assets will be between two and three 'basis points' (a basis point is 0.01 of one per cent, or 1/10,000) for assets held in a major market such as any of the 'Group of Seven' leading economic powers and other principal developed markets. For assets held in emerging markets the typical cost will vary depending on how easily custody services can be supplied on the point in the country concerned. For emerging markets where there are few local problems, the cost will be around 10–15 basis points, whereas for emerging markets which present real problems to custodians the cost can be around 30–40 basis points, or even more.

For example, if an investor has a portfolio of assets with a market value of £10 million, and holds the assets in a major market such as the UK, France, Germany or the US, the cost of a custodian handling these assets would be around between £2000–£3000 per annum, although in practice the cost would probably be higher, as a portfolio of £1 million is a small one which would not allow the global custodian to make many savings deriving from economies of scale. On the other hand, the cost of providing a custody service to a £1 million portfolio held in an emerging market might vary from around £10,000 annually to £40,000: a considerable increase, which would in effect represent for the investor an additional risk of holding assets in emerging markets.

The services typically covered in this fee would include the principal services now associated with custody, namely:

- safe custody of all securities documentation and all monies;
- income collection (e.g. collection of dividends);
- relaying of details of corporate actions (e.g. AGMs, voting).

An additional fee may be charged for handling additional functions, such as proxy voting, tax reclamation, securities lending and so on. As well as the above fee based around the market value of the assets held, the global custodian would also charge a fee for each settlement transaction undertaken on behalf of the investor. There is often considerable room for negotiation here; clearly, a global custodian that has to enact many transactions on behalf of the investor could not expect to charge the same 'per transaction' fee as one that only had to enact a few transactions each week.

Where a fund under management is substantial, the associated fees accruing to the global custodian can also be high; too high, perhaps, for investors who are intent on keeping costs down. But – to reiterate a point already raised in Chapter 2 – it is important to remember at this point that a good global custodian can in effect *make* money for the investor, by extending services which help the investor to collect revenue from its investments, and by maximizing the efficiency of the handling of all these services.

An efficient income collection service, for example, can obviously help to bring the investor more revenue than an inefficient service, as the sooner the dividends are in the investor's bank account, the sooner they can start earning interest. Even a relatively straightforward service, such as relaying details of corporate actions can have an impact on fund performance. For example, providing the investor with timely warning of a crucial AGM can enable it to vote (whether in person or by proxy) at the meeting and thereby influence decisions which may have important repercussions for the fund.

Tax reclamation is an even more important service as far as bringing revenue to the investor is concerned. Some global custodians are somewhat complacent about this service; they sometimes give the impression of believing that tax reclamation is automatic where double taxation agreements are in place. Sometimes it is, but often it isn't, and even where it is, the establishment of a good local contact between the custodian (or sub-custodian) and the local tax office can greatly speed the process of getting the tax back and relaying it to the investor's account, where – again – it can start earning interest.

Of all the services provided by a global custodian, securities lending offers the most potential for generating extra revenue. Too many investors are unnecessarily cautious about using it, often feeling that the securities lent would represent too high a risk. As the custodian arranging the loan will always arrange for collateral – in the form of cash or shares – to be deposited with the lender by the borrower before the loan takes place, the risk involved should be small. Fees for lending securities vary considerably, depending on the extent to which the security in question is in demand at the time. A security not particularly difficult to obtain might earn the lender around five to ten basis points; one which is heavily in demand might earn as much as 200 basis points: a useful return if you're lending, say, £10 million worth of securities!

Overall, I would advise that when you select a global custodian, you should take care to look carefully at your levels of business and the breadth and range of services you'll need, and ensure that the different candidates quote for those service levels. That way, you will protect yourself as far as is feasible against the custodian having the opportunity to charge you more in the future. Remember, too, that you may have to take a business decision over whether to opt for a less expensive global custodian who may not be very good at earning you additional revenue, and a more expensive one who will. Be prepared to negotiate hard over what you are being charged for settlement transactions, and take particular care with what your prospective global custodian is planning to charge you for handling your assets in the very emerging markets where you are hoping that, by taking on additional risk, you can also earn better-than-average returns. You obviously want the bulk of those returns to go into your fund rather than into the pockets of your global custodian. And what's more, that is a desire to which you are perfectly entitled.

CONCLUSION

In this chapter I considered the crucial issue of the cost aspects of using an external global custodian. I looked at typical ways in which global custodians charge for their services and suggested the level of importance which should be accorded to costs when a global custodian is selected.

I also gave consideration to the crucial issues of those global custody services which make a prime contribution to generating revenue for the investor. In this respect I looked in particular at income collection, notification of details of corporate actions, tax reclamation and securities lending.

WORKING WITH A GLOBAL CUSTODIAN ON A DAY-TO-DAY BASIS

6

INTRODUCTION

The essence of good global custody is the quality of the relationship between the investor and the custodian. As with all relationships, its quality is, almost by definition, dependent on both sides of the participation doing what they should be doing.

From the global custodian's perspective, the onus of obligation is clear enough, and fundamentally straightforward. The custodian must fulfil the terms of its brief according to the contract it has signed with the investor. This contract should, indeed, be regarded by the custodian as something of a working document: like this book itself, it should be something for the desk-top, not for the bookshelf.

But the investor cannot imagine that the onus of responsibility for making the global custody relationship work falls on the shoulders of the custodian alone. Just as with many other things in life, one can only expect to get good things out if one puts good things in. To come down to specifics, an investor needs to pay attention to all of the following issues on a day-to-day basis if it wants to make the very most of the relationship with the global custodian.

● The investor must set up reliable methods for receiving from the custodian information relating to all relevant matters for which the custodian is responsible. Where information is time-critical, such as in the case of information relating to corporate actions, the information must be relayed to the investor in sufficient time for the investor to consider the implications of the information and to act on it.

- To ensure that its assured income (i.e. income deriving from its holdings) is received from the custodian on time and that channels exist for the rapid conveyance of this income to the investor's own clients (if applicable).

- To ensure that income obtained from other sources (e.g. from securities lending and tax reclamation) is maximized.

- Generally to ensure that the global custodian abides by the service level agreement and contractual arrangements it has concluded with the investor.

- To seek to create a genuine *partnership* with the global custodian, with both sides benefiting from the partnership.

It is essential that the investor adopts a determined approach to fulfilling all the above objectives. Global custodians are no different from any other organization in that they are run by people and it is a fact of human nature that after the excitement of winning a new client has passed – and after the 'honeymoon' period of the new custodian-client relationship is over – there is a tendency for the level of service slowly to worsen, or at least to cease being continuously improved.

Ultimately, the only way to prevent this slackening of standards in the provision of the global custody service is for the investor to take full control of the relationship and to monitor the performance of the custodian at all times in a fair but forthright manner.

THE NEED FOR THE INVESTOR TO APPOINT A CUSTODY LIAISON OFFICER

A necessary element of the smooth functioning of the investor/custodian relationship is the appointment by the investor, internally, of a *custody liaison officer*. This person will take charge of the process of monitoring the custodian's activities and channel any queries or complaints directly to the custodian in order that these problems can be dealt with efficiently and speedily. The role of custody liaison officer need not encompass the entire duties of the member of staff in question, but it should certainly be regarded as an important part of the his or her duties.

It is essential to have a specific person appointed to carry out this function rather than to have, in effect, all the investor's staff who deal with the custodian's staff on a day-to-day basis carrying out the role. The reasons for this are:

(a) when a custody liaison officer has been appointed, he or she can obtain an overview of the entire custodian/investor relationship and will be well placed to know whether a query or complaint is a real problem or just a temporary irritation;

(b) the custody liaison officer can ensure that real problems are directed to the custodian at a senior level, rather than being directed to members of the custodian's operational staff, who should be left to pursue the specializations for which they are qualified. In any case, if the query concerns the inattentiveness or other less than top-quality performance by a member of the operational staff, they are hardly likely to be the correct person to deal with the complaint.

Most custodians will also appoint someone who will oversee the relationship with investors. This person is usually known as the client (or customer) relationship manager, and it is with this person that the custody liaison officer should deal.

As can readily be imagined, there is little point in the custodian appointing a relationship officer if that officer does not have the authority to effect, where necessary, radical changes to the way the custodian does business. The investor should require that where changes are necessary, they take place quickly and smoothly.

Although there is no *necessary* reason why a custody liaison officer should not be involved with the custodian on a day-to-day basis, there is a case for appointing an officer who is not involved in this way. The reason is that such a person will bring a greater degree of objectivity to the process of overviewing the custodian's performance. Furthermore, as often applies in the business world, there may be advantages deriving from the lack of personal involvement the officer has with the problem under discussion. Whether or not the officer is personally involved in working with the custodian on a day-to-day basis, it is essential that he or she establishes lines of communication with staff who are so involved. These lines of communication should be set up to ensure rapid relaying of details of problems that may arise in the relationship.

THE IDEAL WORKING RELATIONSHIP BETWEEN
THE INVESTOR AND THE CUSTODIAN

It is important that the investor exercises vigilance over the activities of the custodian; the ideal working relationship should not be based on a situation of constant conflict between the investor and the custodian, but rather on a collaborative relationship where the central aim is to get the job done properly. However, the relationship will only be collaborative where the custodian is delivering a quality of service that meets the investor's expectations.

THE NEED FOR A PROCEDURE TO DEAL
WITH DISSATISFACTION

When the investor and custodian sign their agreement, they should also decide on a procedure for resolving disputes. Some investors may even want to include these provisions in the contract, although that might be seen as making problems more likely, by enshrining within the body of the agreement the fact that they are expected.

Certainly, where the dispute resolution procedure is *not* agreed within the contract, it should be agreed early on in the working relationship to deal with investor dissatisfaction with the custodian's service. A typical procedure would include the following stages, with the procedure only moving on to the next stage if the problem persists.

Figure 6.1 Dispute resolution procedure

> **Stage 1:** verbal discussion between investor's custody liaison officer and custodian's relationship manager;
>
> **Stage 2:** further verbal discussion, with the custody liaison officer pointing out that the problem is still unresolved;
>
> **Stage 3:** verbal discussion of problem between a senior member of investor's organization and senior member of custodian's organization;
>
> **Stage 4:** preliminary written complaint;
>
> **Stage 5:** further written complaint;
>
> **Stage 6:** termination of relationship.

The termination of the relationship is a draconian step and will involve the investor in considerable inconvenience. It is included here for the sake of completeness, but should only be invoked if there is no alternative.

Where the investor is an investment management organization which invests funds on behalf of a number of clients, the investor will often be dealing with custodians who have been appointed by the clients rather than by the investor. However, this does not mean that the investor should be prepared to accept lower standards from its clients' custodians than if it had appointed the custodians itself. The clients have given the investor a mandate to maximize the return on funds held on their behalf; the investor would be failing in its duty if it did not strive to obtain the best service it could from its clients' custodians.

One large and highly successful Scottish investment management organization which works with numerous custodians, most of whom have been appointed by its own clients, told me:

> 'We may not have appointed many of our custodians ourselves, but we treat them as if we had. After all, our clients would have every right to complain to us if revenue from their assets was not being maximized, and efficient global custody is an important element in maximizing this revenue. Not only do we monitor the performance of the custodians with considerable energy, but we are perfectly prepared to recommend to our clients that they terminate a custodian if we feel there is nothing to be gained by prolonging the relationship. I don't think we are unreasonable in the demands we place upon custodians, but I won't deny that we regard it as essential to our professionalism to be tough.'

An interesting procedure practised by this investor is to compile monthly books on the quality of service provided by the various custodians with whom the investor deals. These books, which are circulated to clients and to all the custodians involved as well as within the investor's organization, represent powerful incentives for custodians, as well as useful guides for clients on how well their custodians are performing. In the books, the investor grades the performance of the custodians from one (excellent) to five (very poor) on six criteria, namely:

- settlement performance
- quality of booking
- performance of computer system
- stock discrepancies (i.e. the accuracy with which the custodian is monitoring stock held on behalf of the investor)
- income collection and payment
- overall performance.

Investors that use multiple custodians may wish to produce custodian evaluation books which judge custodians according to these and/or other criteria which the investor feels to be pertinent.

Note that, in order for the exercise to be fair (and to avoid the small but not unrealistic possibility that a maligned custodian may regard an adverse book as grounds for libel) the evaluation should as far as feasible be based on objective rather than subjective factors.

COMMON PROBLEM AREAS

Problems with the provision of global custody services on a day-to-day basis can occur across all aspects of the service. However, experience shows that some problems are more likely than others. In particular, the following areas tend to be especially sensitive. As a result, the investor would be well advised to mention to the custodian, at the start of the relationship, that the investor would be pleased if the custodian were to pay particular attention to these areas.

Provision by the custodian to the investor of names of all operational staff and their direct telephone numbers

It is important that this information is not only provided by the custodian to the investor at the outset, but also that the information is updated regularly and that the investor is informed about staff changes and changes to staff responsibility.

Avoidance of unanswered telephone calls

The investor can reasonably expect the custodian's telephones to be staffed at all times when the custodian's office is open, and ideally, by a person rather than voicemail. Voicemails are generally regarded within the global custody industry as an extremely unsatisfactory means of communication. The idea which some executives have (and, it must be said, especially young executives), that voicemails are a substitute for a real person is not only a mistaken notion, but a dangerously mistaken one, at least in so far as the chance of the global custodian keeping the relationship with the investor intact is concerned. Few things are more infuriating than for a busy investor to ring with an urgent query on which he or she wants to get closure rapidly and to find that there is no-one available, only a voicemail. But even a voicemail is better than a telephone that is completely unanswered, and there are too many of those in the global custody industry, too.

Telephone calls not returned

Just as with unanswered telephone calls, few things are more annoying to an investor than to have calls not returned. Of course, this is a courtesy that also applies in the other direction.

Rudeness or flippancy on the part of the custodian's staff

This problem can damage an investor/custodian relationship with alarming ease. A scarcely less annoying subset of this problem is the person who answers the telephone while in the middle of a jocular conversation with a colleague, and is consequently laughing or sniggering when answering the phone. An investor is entitled to expect complete professionalism from the custodian's staff in terms of telephone manner.

Queries not attended to and/or resolved with careful and genuine attentiveness and thoughtful haste

The investor can expect the custodian to attend to and/or resolve queries with maximum speed, which in practice should mean within the same business day in most cases.

Lapses in quality of core service and additional service provision

Any lapse in these areas is potentially extremely serious for an investor, which can reasonably expect (and demand) the custodian to take every effort to maintain the highest level of service in both the SMAC services and additional services.

CONCLUSION

In this chapter, I emphasized that the essence of good global custody is the quality of the relationship between the investor and the custodian. I made the crucially important point that the quality of this relationship depends on both participants doing what they should be doing.

I set down key issues which need to be attended to if the investor is to make the most of its relationship with the global custodian. I also looked at the importance of appointing a custody liaison officer and considered how the day-to-day working relationship between custodian and investor ought to operate.

Finally, I considered common problem areas and suggested how these might be avoided.

GLOBAL CUSTODY TECHNOLOGY

7

INTRODUCTION

In this chapter, 'technology' refers to computer-based information technology used by custodians and investors. 'Electronic information' refers to information stored or communicated digitally: that is, in computer-readable format.

These definitions of technology and electronic information do not include the telephone or facsimile machine, because these use what is, clearly, a less advanced technology. In practical terms, the telephone plays an absolutely essential role in the global custody service and the facsimile also plays a crucial role here – many would say *too* crucial a role. The point is that while there is no substitute for the telephone as an aid to remote voice communications – although in future we are likely to see a higher proportion of voice communications being undertaken by video phone systems that interface digitally with PCs – the facsimile machine is certainly used more extensively by custodians than is ideal. It is not very secure; anybody who sees the fax can read it, and it is not practicable to encrypt facsimile messages. Furthermore, facsimile communications are not transmitted in digital format, which means that they have to be scanned before they can be digitized and put into a computer. This greatly limits their usefulness. Another important point is that the facsimile transmission, if lost, cannot be replaced without requesting a new transmission to be made by the original organization.

There is no doubt that the future of global custody depends very substantially on the future of technology. There is no mystery as to why this is the case. As Chris Rees, a director of leading London-based financial technology consultancy Charteris told me:

'The whole process of domestic or global custody hinges substantially on a large number of processes being regularly completed with complete accuracy and great speed, and then repeated on a continual basis. Handling these kind of processes is precisely what computers are best at doing. Furthermore, custodians will typically be handling the administrative requirements of portfolios containing hundreds of stocks and other types of securities: only a computer can handle the complex processes relating to all these stocks with the levels of accuracy and speed required. These reasons not only explain why custodians need technology to do their jobs properly, but also why competition over technology is a major element of competitiveness among custodians.'

ATTITUDES TOWARDS TECHNOLOGY HELD
BY CUSTODIANS

Unfortunately, not all domestic or global custodians view technology in such an important light as Chris Rees does. Even today, manual processing of global custody activity is still very much a feature of the international securities industry. This is particularly so in custodians located in emerging markets, but it is true of some custodian in some developed countries, too. In 1997 I undertook a consultancy project for a well-known American bank at one of its major UK offices. The settlement and transaction processing procedure was still manual, and so cumbersome that a team of about 12 custody back-office staff considered that they were doing well if they could process a grand total of 20 transactions in a day.

As one might expect, even in modern scenarios where most custodian banks are much more automated than this, custodian banks still need to retain staff who know how to handle processes manually, because there is always the danger that the computer-based resources might stop operating for some reason.

However, the general trend is for custodians of all kinds to transfer more and more of their functionality onto computers and to rely very heavily on the computer system to undertake the burden of work. I have already mentioned how the pressure for a custodian to spend substantial sums of money on its computer resources in order to maximize their effectiveness, accuracy and speed, is a major issue in why the custody industry has seen so many mergers and shake-outs in recent years. By no means every custodian, even one that is relatively profitable, is prepared to make the substantial technological investments required.

And so some custodians try to get by with the existing technology, while others adopt the somewhat cynical view that it is cheaper to continue to operate a substantially manual system than to invest for the future.

WHY SHOULD TECHNOLOGY MATTER
TO A CUSTODIAN?

In global custody, and on both sides of the global custody relationship, over-caution on technology spend always turns out to be false economy sooner or later. This is not to imply that wasting money on global custody technology makes sense to anybody, but the issue here is not that one should be indiscriminate in spending money on technology, but that one should be *wise* about it. And there really is no avoiding the simple fact that it is not possible to provide, or indeed receive, a truly dynamic, well-organized, speedy and accurate global custody service to investors unless one has state-of-the-art technology in place.

Furthermore, the use of such technology can dramatically reduce the risk which every custodian has to bear in carrying out the custody service. For one thing, technology will permit the creation of a reliable 'audit trail', that is, a record of every transaction and every process undertaken by the system in question. Such an audit trail makes it far more difficult for fraudsters to carry out their activities, because they will need to key in their personal code numbers or code-words into a terminal to get access to it in the first place and this access can be recorded.

Technology also helps to prevent mistakes caused by inadvertent oversight or incompetence, because the system can be set with certain parameters and no transaction outside those parameters will be permitted. General security can also be maximized by the use of subtle aspects of the program: for example, many programs which allow cash payments to be made electronically to remote accounts do not operate unless two separate code-words have been keyed into a terminal. This means that every such transaction must be seen and authorized by two separate people if it is to take place.

Another big advantage of using technology is that it can help to solve the failings of the human memory. Once a computer has been taught to remember something or been programmed to issue a reminder, it can't forget this because the item to be remembered is built into the program and is in essence part of the computer's operation. The human brain, as we all know, is far less reliable in its memory capacity.

We have already seen how extremely important the custodian's role is in every aspect of handling the administrative requirements of a portfolio, and how this role is especially important in the handling of certainly functions which will cause the investor loss (which the custodian would typically have to make up) if the process is not handled properly. Obvious examples are the rights issue and scrip issue. Computers are in an excellent position to remind the custodian's staff of corporate actions that are likely to be coming up and then to keep issuing reminders to the staff until everything has been done and completed and the application to benefit from the corporate action has been dispatched and received by the company in question.

TECHNOLOGY FOR COMMUNICATION BETWEEN THE CUSTODIAN AND EXTERNAL PARTIES

In addition to the importance of technology's role for keeping accurate records of processes going through the custodian's in-house systems and for reminding the custodian's staff of actions that must be taken, technology also plays a crucial role in facilitating communications between the custodian and external parties, who would typically include:

- investors
- brokers
- stock exchanges
- regulatory authorities (who may need information to be supplied to them in order that the custodian comply with regulatory provisions)
- sub-custodians.

Looking at the broad picture, information sent by custodians to external parties can be sent in one of four ways.

1 By voice over the telephone

The telephone is an instantaneous and convenient means of communication, and one with which people are thoroughly familiar.

However, its usefulness as a means of relaying complex information is severely limited by the short attention span people have when listening to information that is extensive and detailed rather than inherently interesting, and by the necessity for the recipient to write down the information. These problems also apply to information relayed in face-to-face meetings.

That said, the telephone is the ideal means for the investor or the custodian to relay (or request) answers to small but important queries arising from any aspect of the global custody process. The element of personal contact in a telephone conversation is essential for the delivery of global custody services and to the creation of a satisfactory and mutually helpful rapport between custodian and investor.

If an investor gives a custodian an instruction over the telephone, the custodian will usually require that this is confirmed in writing within a short period (usually not more than 48 hours).

2 By post

The efficiency of this method depends on the effectiveness of the post. This may not be a serious problem for domestic post in a developed country (although there are exceptions to this, such as the poor state of the system in Italy), but it can be for cross-border post, where general unreliability or severe delays may make this an unrealistic option, especially if the information is being posted from an emerging market to a developed market.

Another drawback with information being sent by post is that if the information needs to be input into the investor's in-house computer system, the paper-based information must be input manually, or via an image processor. Whichever method is used, there will be this additional stage in handling the information.

3 By facsimile

This has the advantages of the voice telephone link without the disadvantages of the recipient's short attention span. It is widely used by investors and custodians as a method of communicating detailed information. Its popularity results from its effectiveness for the task in hand, the fact that it is comparatively inexpensive, the widespread availability of fax machines and the ease with which they can be operated.

There are, however, other drawbacks to the use of the fax in addition to the ones mentioned above. Transmissions are often unsuccessful if there is any slight problem with the communications system, and both sender and recipient are at the mercy of the quality, or otherwise, of the national or cross-border communications system involved. Furthermore, fax paper is notoriously flimsy and often comes out of the machine like a scroll, although many machines circumvent this problem by printing on flat sheets of ordinary paper.

A further problem is that fax transmissions give no opportunity for the communication to be interactive. While the information is being sent, the recipient cannot request further information, specify the information more precisely, or even change the information request completely. Fax transmissions also have the disadvantage that the information must usually be input manually or via an image processor into the investor's in-house computer system, where this is required.

4 Electronic information

This avoids the problems inherent in the above methods of communicating information. Here, the means used is electronic data which is communicated across leased or proprietary telephone lines.

Apart from the speed and accuracy of electronic communications, it carries with it the huge advantage that the electronic communication process can be *fully interactive* between the custodian's computer terminal and that of the external party. Such interactive, real-time communications, making use of the computer's ability to keep an accurate, second-by-second record of everything that is going on, represents what might be termed the highest state of evolution of business communications.

Electronic information also offers the great advantage that it can be readily (or instantly) reconfigured into a format suitable for storage and processing within the investor's own in-house system. It also offers a high degree of security. For example, many interbank messages relating to custody payment instructions are sent via the SWIFT network, whose security (and vast level of activity, with more than $1 trillion being paid via the system every working day) are alike legendary.

Against these undoubted benefits, however, must be set the relatively high cost of the technology compared with the voice telephone or the fax. However, in the custody business, as in other businesses, the cost of the technology must be considered in relation to the benefits the technology would bring.

5 The Internet

I do not yet know how important the Internet is going to be as a means for relaying global custody information, but I do know that everybody in the industry is talking about it. Global custody and the Internet are linked in the minds of many experts on the industry, and for this reason I want to look at it in some detail.

GLOBAL CUSTODY AND THE INTERNET

The Internet is arguably the most important new communications system that has been developed since the Second World War. Most other communication systems which we use today were already established from a technological perspective earlier in the twentieth century or even earlier. The telephone, for example, traces its origins to 1876; it is easy to forget that by the 1880s there were already hundreds of telephone subscribers in New York City. The facsimile (fax) machine, use of which has also expanded at a prodigious rate in recent years so that most businesses have one, as do many private households, is substantially the same technology invented in the 1930s. (Incidentally, the enormous proliferation of the fax machine started in Japan, where the complexity of the Japanese written language made the fax the perfect method for sending written communications over a wire.)

The Internet is an international network of telecommunications systems and servers which interconnect in order to produce what is very much like the international 'web' that has become the accepted way of describing it. People gain access to this web through their personal computers, which typically interface via a data communications line to an Internet service provider (ISP) which is geared up to act as a node on the web, or else go direct to the recipient.

What makes the Internet important is not so much its technological innovativeness but rather its sheer scale. The only areas where it is technologically of particular interest are the speed of its international connections and the remarkable configuration of Internet search engines which enable these engines to search a prodigious databank of international material and references in a matter of seconds. This is achieved through all this material being stored in relation to various key words which are instantly picked up by the search engines' servers.

At one level the Internet is simply like a gigantic on-line library, giving the user access to all web sites. These web sites are specific nodes containing information, usually presented in a deliberately attractive and user-friendly way. Unlike a library, the information is not necessarily ordered in a particularly convenient fashion, which is why when you make a search for a particular word or phrase you are as likely to receive extremely unhelpful material as helpful material. However, many Internet searches are a great success merely because one or two pieces of information become available which would not otherwise be so, due to the fact that the user would not otherwise know how to find them.

Furthermore, material available through the Internet is extremely 'topical'. Web sites are updated regularly and it is perfectly possible for a search to reveal material that was only posted to the Internet a few minutes earlier. Retrieving information from a library, however, inevitably involves a considerable time lag between the setting down of the information on paper and the information being available.

Another major advantage of the Internet is that it permits users to 'download' whatever information takes their fancy and either store this information on their own computer system or else print out copies. There is an almost unimaginable range of information available via the Internet for downloading, from names and e-mail addresses of famous persons or old friends, judgments issued by law courts – especially in notorious cases – recreational information such as screenplays of famous movies and an enormous amount of commercial information. For many companies, the most obvious commercial use of the Internet is simply to provide a highly cost-effective advertisement about their products and services. The advertisement can be comparatively lengthy because there is no price to pay for transmitting the details over the broadcast medium: the user's own telephone bill pays for the access time.

As an international communications system, the Internet is particularly interesting in that it is not governed by any regulatory authority. This makes it highly attractive to people living in countries where the telecommunications system is poor due to problems with the national infrastructure and also in countries where the government has a strict control of other communications and broadcast systems.

The popularity of the Internet is undeniable. At the time of writing, about 148 million people worldwide have regular access to the Internet. The volume of Internet traffic is doubling every 100 days. Similarly reliable estimates suggest that by the year 2002, about 320 million people will have regular access to the Internet. This will be equivalent to about 4 per cent of the world's population. When one considers that a large part of this population are not living in technologically developed countries, it is clear that in developed countries a significant proportion of the population will be using the Internet by the early years of the twenty-first century.

What exactly do users think of the Internet and why do they use it?

A major survey of Internet users, carried out in April 1998 by a leading management consultancy, states that 93 per cent of Internet users said that they found their access to the World Wide Web 'indispensable', while a similar proportion said that they found the use of e-mail also to be indispensable. The survey also found that the Internet is as popular for leisure purposes as for work purposes.

Indeed, as more and more people use their own individual PC as their central tool in the workplace, and also the central tool for organizing their leisure and professional life combined, the old barriers between work and play are obviously starting to erode. This is especially true, bearing in mind the fact that more and more people – especially in high-powered professional jobs – are not working regular hours but are working when they travel and also spending a fair amount of work time at home. This development is unquestionably being accelerated by the increasing use of laptop and palm top PCs, which have considerable amounts of power and which are of course entirely portable. Today's personal computers are, increasingly, genuinely personal.

Just as the number of Internet users is surging, so is the number of Internet 'hosts', that is, web sites put onto the Internet by a wide range of organizations which wish to communicate with users.

The Internet's popularity is not difficult to explain. It is easy to use – for very good commercial reasons, web site providers almost fall over themselves to make their sites user-friendly – and it is normally readily accessible. The problems which most users experience at some stage – such as problems of slow access times, occasional impossibility of access and sudden interruptions to Internet service – are due to the burgeoning demand for the service and the fact that the technology is sometimes overloaded as a result. In the future it seems certain that these problems will be substantially solved.

For many people in business, and especially those engaged in the genuinely global custody industry, which places so many travel demands on its senior executives that an ability to keep up one's spirits when faced with yet another hotel room and yet another client dinner night is a key professional requirement, the most fundamental benefit of the Internet is its sheer *portability*. A portable PC can literally be plugged into any telephone socket around the world, with Internet access provided within a matter of seconds. An American custodian visiting Europe to meet with top management of some sub-custodian or other can obtain access to his or her e-mail messages via the Internet as easily as if he or she were at home. Indeed, many telephone providers encourage this use by offering customers a favourable or even local rate for overseas Internet access time. Similarly, major international hotels are increasingly siting telephone sockets close to desks in their rooms. Some even provide business centres where desktop and portable PCs can be borrowed and Internet access time paid for.

The portable PC will also interface with every other benefit of the Internet: the enormous global library of information is available the instant the connection is made. It is difficult to imagine a more potentially powerful communications tool.

The Internet applications I've discussed so far are very much one-way communications: meaning that the user is obtaining information rather than providing it. Of course, when a user responds to an e-mail message, he or she is providing information. But this is a static type of communication and not normally conducted in real time. The Internet has unquestionably proven its usefulness as a means of disseminating information from a wide variety of sources to users: this application will ensure its continued growth. But what about its use as a means of *interactive* communications? This is a matter to which we now turn.

The Internet was first developed in the late-1970s as a way for university libraries to make information available over data communications lines to interested persons. From the beginning, it was conceived of as an international public access computer network linking computers from these educational institutions to computers operated by users. The system's growth into an international network in which millions of web site providers and users participate is easy to understand with hindsight, but at the time would have seemed merely science fiction. It is almost as if the computer database of your local library had started to run riot and seek to connect itself to all the PCs in the world.

The notion of public access to the Internet was central to its genesis and has remained central to its operation since then. The very point that *anybody* with a PC and an ISP can, in principle, access anything on the Internet is enshrined in the whole concept.

But it is inevitable that some web providers – and an increasing number as time goes by – will want to find ways of communicating with specially favoured users while also maintaining a link to *any* interested persons. These specially favoured customers will, almost by definition, be people who the web site providers see as good business prospects. These prospects will probably want to see the same or similar type of information provided to anybody *but may wish to reply in an interactive way to the web site provider.*

This is exactly the position that a typical global custodian will be in. On the one hand, it will want to advertise and otherwise promote its services to any investors (and of course particularly to any major institutional investors) who might be surfing the web. On the other hand, it will also want to use the Internet as an initiator for interactive contact with surfers who have a special status, such as customers.

One obvious way of arranging for this interactive contact to take place is for the customer to reply by telephone or fax, thereby enabling the web site provider to establish the bona fide nature of the caller. For example, a custodian could say whatever it wanted to say about itself in its web site, but it would only give information about a particular customer's account once it had established the credentials of the customer in question.

However, in practice, restricting the interactive communications based around the Internet to the telephone or fax is not really very good business, for the following reasons.

- It obliges users to go to the trouble of making a telephone call or sending a fax: something they might find too time-consuming to do. This is, one might add, especially the case in many financial applications, such as FOREX, where prevailing prices do not prevail for very long, and might even have changed by the time the fax lands on the trader's desk.
- It restricts users to interacting with the organization in real time during office hours. Outside office hours the user can still leave a message, but this would not be acted on until the counterparty's office opens.
- Use of a telephone or fax involves the user in additional charges which they might not wish to pay.
- Use of a telephone or fax necessitates relatively complex secu-

rity authorization in any case and will tend to slow the process down even further.

Faced with these problems, it is not surprising that custodians – and their investor clients – have given careful thought to the possibilities of conducting secure, private interactive communications over the Internet.

There is a great deal to be said for the Internet as an interactive communications medium. The breadth of information that can be communicated is very substantial, the speed of communications can be close to instantaneous, the screen interface provides considerable opportunities for displaying feedback, and the very nature of the PC makes the conversation private. Furthermore, a counterparty can be selected with enormous facility and speed.

Additionally, the interactive communications facility can be integrated into an existing desktop facility and can be triggered by simply clicking on an icon with a mouse or pressing a key. There is no need to shut down an application, the interactive communication via the Internet can simply sit 'on top' of it. Furthermore, a complete and comprehensive record can readily be kept of the interactive conversation and can be provided as proof of anything agreed via the two counterparties.

Indeed, there is only one reason why the Internet is not already being used extensively for interactive communications.

This reason is the problem of security.

The Internet security challenge

The problem of the security of an Internet communication is a formidable one. By definition, we should only regard it as applying to a 'valuable' communication: that is, any message which is directly or indirectly worth money.

Obviously, a vast proportion of messages communicated one

way across the Internet to a user may be interesting for the user, highly informative and may in fact give the user ideas and opportunities for conducting valuable business. But this type of message – that is, the standard information material available over the Internet – is not the kind that concerns me here. I am focusing on messages which have an immediate, or almost immediate monetary value.

We are also talking about messages which are valuable by virtue of their *exclusivity*. Many messages sent over the Internet will not necessarily have an immediate monetary value, but will have some other special value attached to them. For example, a communication across the Internet from a doctor to a patient is unlikely to have a financial value for the patient – indeed it probably won't – but it certainly is a message which must be kept confidential.

Similarly, if a global custodian is proposing to conduct a service over the Internet – that is, a service which actually *delivers custodian facilities* rather than merely provides information to users – the communication will naturally need to be kept secret.

What I am therefore, talking about is receiving and delivering a secret message across a medium designed for open and public access.

The best analogy for the type of security arrangement we are discussing here is the notion of a scrambled telephone call. This is a technique whereby a telephone call is made impossible or difficult to access by unauthorized persons by the electric pulses of the message being rearranged in the outgoing handset and therefore sent across the communication system in a form that cannot be overheard. At the receiving handset the message is scrambled back into standard format and consequently can be understood by the recipient.

Scrambled telephone messages are still used in some governmental areas requiring the utmost secrecy, but generally improvements to telephone technology have greatly reduced the incidence of crossed lines which were one reason why scrambling was regarded as so important.

The Internet also makes use of telecommunications systems – especially the major international telephone lines – and so the analogy is complete. What is required in order to carry out this objective is:

(a) some way of scrambling the communication so as to make it impossible to read, and ideally also impossible to interfere with or corrupt;

(b) a technique for ensuring that only bona fide persons can send or receive messages.

The particular importance of this need to scramble messages and consequently make them impossible to read by unauthorized persons arises from the fact that no organization can control which route a message takes as it crosses the Internet. The route will depend on traffic volumes and is not predictable.

Another crucial element in the security process is for the bona fide user of the system to authorize his or her use of it in much the same way as a user of a bank network has to authorize his or her bona fide nature using a bank card and a PIN. This authorization process is essential because there is not much point in 'scrambling' the Internet communication if the message then appears on the screen of the PC which is being used by someone other than the bona fide person.

In practice, Internet communications are made secure using a dual element process. First, the *authentication* of the incoming party is established using a digital certificate which enables the party to prove it is bona fide by writing what is called a digital signature. The digital certificate is some kind of electronic token which provides specific authentication for the user.

The second stage of the process provides *authorization* to specific data to which the incoming party has legitimate access. This authorization will typically be provided by the use of user identification and a password.

Increasingly, digital certification is being provided by smart cards (also known as chip cards). These have the big advantage that they contain a microchip. Consequently, a considerable amount of data can be stored in the chip for a variety of authentication and message recognition features. Furthermore, smart cards are making their way more and more into everyday life in electronic purses, loyalty cards and credit cards, and so many users will already be familiar with them. It is also relatively simple to exploit the ever-increasing processing power of smart card chips for public key encryption and designing digital signatures.

The essence of any Internet security system is encryption: that is, precisely the same technique used to render secure other types of information sent across an electronic communications system. There is, however, one additional safeguard which almost all Internet security systems feature. This is the 'firewall'.

The term 'firewall' sounds intimidating, but merely describes a barrier between an organization's internal computer network and the Internet, with the purpose of the barrier being only to allow authorized traffic to pass. Authorization is based on a set of rules which have the total effect of confining acceptable incoming traffic to certain specified criteria. These criteria usually relate to such matters as: acceptable incoming Internet services, acceptable Internet web site addresses and acceptable hosts. Some firewalls allow users to check and even modify the rules whenever they wish to do so.

Clearly, a firewall is only as good as the rules relating to what it can and cannot accept. Generally, firewalls are a highly effective way of protecting a network and sensitive information from malicious attack from outside services. The point is that *only access which is explicitly permitted will be allowed to come in through the firewall*. There are no ifs, no buts, no grey areas, no opportunity for smooth-talking persuasion, no tricks and no subjective interpretations. A message is either accepted by virtue of it meeting all the acceptance criteria, or it is rejected. The technical elements of firewalls are not an important subject to us, because an organization needs specialized assistance with setting up a firewall and should leave this task to knowledgeable professionals. Suffice it to say that there are many different types of firewalls, from straightforward routers which examine packet communications coming in from web site providers, to software packages which operate at the application level. As one might expect, the more thorough a firewall is, the more complete the security it provides.

Firewalls are extremely important as ways of screening an organization's internal network from any kind of Internet communication. The beauty of them is that it is not necessary for the user to specify every type of *unacceptable* message: all the user has to do is specify the *acceptable* messages. This is ideal for organizations which do not want their staff to use the Internet for private leisure reasons during working hours just as it is ideal for organizations which want to screen out all types of other messages.

Firewalls play an essential role in defending an organization such as a global custodian from people trying to gain illicit access to its internal computer network (intranet) via the Internet. Firewalls provide this protection in a variety of ways, but mainly by concealing the individual addresses of users of the intranet and thereby restricting the would-be hacker to seeing information released by the firewall: that is, information which is freely available and not confidential.

Firewalls also play a key role in helping to protect an organization against viruses which it might otherwise download from the Internet. The point is that downloading any data from the Internet is bound to be risky for an organisation because there is always the danger that the information might contain a virus. Obviously, the disruptive individuals who spread viruses will try to conceal the virus within some information which may be expected to be appealing to a person browsing the web. Most Internet service providers have techniques for detecting suspect information and will post warnings to accompany it to persuade users from downloading it. Merely viewing the data on the screen is not a problem, the problem arises if you try to download it.

Firewalls are, in this respect what might be seen as a first line of defence: they restrict what comes into the organization to data which has been previously agreed as acceptable. But the firewall alone is not a sufficient defence against viruses: it should be used in conjunction with a good anti-virus package which runs on a PC and which detects viruses and prevents them being loaded onto the PC's hard drive or onto the hard drive of any other hardware.

Firewalls and Internet-based interactive communications security strategy

By way of example, consider how the firewall is part of the security procedures for an interactive communications system via the Internet. I am quoting the example of the configuration for the Internet security procedure at the leading US investment bank Brown Brothers Harriman and Co.

The communication comes in, *in encrypted form*, via the Internet and is authenticated by a digital certificate. At the point of entry to the firewall, which will only accept incoming communications that have been authenticated in this way, the actual authorization of the user to specific data is provided by the user's identity and password. Only if these different elements are in place will the firewall permit the communication to continue.

Once the authenticated, authorized *but still encrypted* communication passes beyond the firewall, it is decoded by the web server using the encryption key. It is then processed within the organization's intranet and the outgoing communication embarks on a journey which is the reverse of the incoming communication. That is, it leaves the intranet, is encrypted using the encryption key and then passes through to the Internet and then on to the counterparty, which will typically have its own authentication and authorization requirements and may also have a firewall in place. The counterparty will also decode the message so that it can be read in the clear (i.e. in decoded form) on the counterparty's screen.

Assuming that all these provisions are in place, there is no reason why the Internet should be any less secure as a communications medium than, say, a standard bank network such as an ATM network.

The final point to make here is that some organizations do not like to use encryption for interactive communications because sometimes, as can be imagined, the very process of encryption tends to make authentication, authorization and passage through the firewall more difficult than it needs to be. However, in general, all these different security elements are used.

Internet security – conclusions

My own conclusions about Internet security are very much in line with those of official bodies such as the UK Department of Trade and Industry (DTI) which has taken considerable efforts to educate organizations about the dangers of security posed by the Internet. The DTI states its conclusions on this front as being as follows.

- The Internet is inherently insecure because it is a public network that has no central management or control.
- A company using the Internet is responsible for the security of its own network and systems.
- There are people on the Internet who are able to attack your computer systems and information and enjoy the challenge of attempting to gain unauthorized access.

- Organizations cannot control the route which a message will take when it crosses the Internet, from, say the UK to the US.
- It is possible for messages across the Internet to be read or modified by unauthorized people.

For an organization to understand to what extent its business is exposed to the risk of Internet security, it needs to consider the following issues:

- the value of the information;
- the harm to the business which could result from a security breach;
- the realistic likelihood of a security breach occurring, taking into account both current threats and existing controls.

The DTI goes on to discuss certain 'dangerous' myths about Internet security. It lists these as being as follows.

- **The service provider is responsible for the security of your information and your connection.** No, it is your responsibility.
- **No one with an Internet connection would want to access information passing over it.** No, there are a number of people who are interested in this information and capable of accessing it.
- **All systems connected to the Internet are secure.** No, many are inherently insecure.
- **No one can divert, copy or modify information as it passes across the Internet.** No, there are people who are capable of doing this.
- **Business financial transactions are safe when transmitted across the Internet.** No, this is only true if you take precautions to protect your information. Internationally agreed technologies for protecting financial transactions over the Internet are emerging and some are now available.

As a final point, it is necessary to emphasize that Internet security is not merely a matter of putting up the electronic shields. It is also necessary to ensure that staff understand the importance of Internet security and adhere to internal procedures relating to this. As Duncan Reid of the computer security organisation Zergo puts it:

> *'With Internet security, as with other types of computer security, you can't just bolt on some security software to the system and expect that to be the total answer to the problem. You must also make sure that your staff are properly educated in the actual use of the software and are motivated to make proper use of it each time rather than try to bypass it in order to avoid the small amount of inconvenience that using computer security software sometimes entails.'*

THE ROLE OF OFFICIAL ELECTRONIC INFORMATION EXCHANGES IN THE MESSAGING PROCESS

The exchange of messages between banks regarding payments, transfers of ownership of securities, by and sell transactions, and details of many other types of information, is an essential part of global custody. Given the large number of banks in the world which practice global or domestic custody (at least 500) and the fact that many of these banks will want to exchange messages with numerous other banks on a given banking day, it is not surprising that official organizations have been created to speed the exchange of electronic information.

One of the best-known organizations is the Society for World-wide Interbank Funds Telecommunications (SWIFT). SWIFT, which handles trillions of dollars of payments transactions every day as well as many other types of messages, is an international consortium famed for the extremely high security of its operations.

169

Unlike most banks themselves and banking organizations, SWIFT has never been broken into by hackers, at least not according to any reliable industry sources. It is so successful that it is nowadays an industry standard for interbank messages as well as an organization for handling these messages.

All global custodians are SWIFT members and, indeed, no investor should consider hiring a global custodian unless it is a member of SWIFT, because otherwise it will not be able easily to offer access to SWIFT facilities. Some smaller banks are SWIFT members but many are not. However, many will be able to offer a SWIFT facility via a global custodian with which they work.

Until the early 1990s, SWIFT had no realistic competition as an organization for facilitating the exchange of interbank messages. However, the past couple of years have seen the rise to prominence of a completely new organization, known as Financial Information Exchange (FIX). Originally founded in 1992, FIX itself and its protocol are becoming increasingly popular. At present its main market is the US, but it is now starting to be used more extensively by custodians and investors outside the US market. There is a general feeling within the global custody industry that FIX has been quicker to look at ways of offering custodians and investors access to straight-through processing (*see* below), and that while the increasing use of the FIX protocol does not present a mortal threat to SWIFT, the combination of FIX with Electronic Trade Confirmation (ETC), leading eventually to the possibility that a custodian or investor will be able to enjoy straight-through processing on any brand of communications network, does indeed present a serious competitive threat to SWIFT. Unfortunately, SWIFT – despite its worldwide impact – has something of a reputation within the industry for bureaucracy and a relatively slow response to major new industry developments. It remains to be seen whether the global custody industry will happily accommodate both SWIFT and FIX, or whether at some stage one of these networks will triumph at the expense of the other.

STRAIGHT-THROUGH PROCESSING

Electronic communications represent the ideal communications method between custodians and external parties; being fast, reliable, capable of being readily recorded and also capable of being included in an audit trail. There is, however, one drawback to electronic communications that involve people; and that is precisely what the drawback is: that people are involved.

People make mistakes, commit oversights, focus on matters which interest them for subjective reasons rather than because the matters are necessarily the most urgent.

Fortunately for the global custody industry and for investors generally, a new form of technique has been developed to facilitate communications between custodians and external parties and leave people as far as possible out of the communications process entirely. Clearly some type of human involvement will be required at the start of the process to input the data (unless this can be done automatically) and to receive the output, but the overall aim is to eliminate human involvement, and therefore human error, from the equation.

This form of processing with no human involvement during the process of transition is known as 'straight-through processing' (STP). It is seen by many as defining the future of global custody technology.

The consultant Chris Rees, who is quoted earlier, is a recognized expert on STP. He has kindly given permission for me to reproduce here his authoritative paper on this technique. This paper, which is written from the investor's viewpoint, now follows.

Straight-through processing and how to achieve it

What is the most tedious, unproductive, unattractive task which the back office of every fund manager faces on a regular basis? Surely reconciliation has no competitors for this title. Reconciling the front office with the back office, the portfolios with the accounting system, the deals with brokers, with custodians, with counterparties of every kind is a necessary evil of the trading environment. Why? Because trade details at all stages of the dealing and settlement cycles are entered by different people at different times, because there is repetitive entry of the same information and because there is too much manual intervention.

Can anything be done to reduce the volume of reconciliation? Yes, straight-through processing can make a material difference. Will reconciliation ever go away? No, reconciliation will always be needed at some level, because even the best managed systems are susceptible to error, because misunderstandings will continue to arise and because no-one should rely on the accuracy of computer systems without external checks, and because there can be genuine differences between counterparties. But straight-through processing offers the opportunity to eliminate re-keying and to effect reconciliation in real time. The benefits are not limited to the reduction in wasted effort and boredom.

Straight-through processing defined

So what is straight-through processing? Simply put, it is the ability to conduct trade confirmation, settlement and reconciliation between the fund manager and its trading partners from initial trade entry through to final settlement electronically, securely and reliably. It depends on the deal being captured once and once only. It embraces Electronic Trade Confirmation (ETC), Electronic Trade Settlement (ETS) and Automated Reconciliation. It can cover securities trading as well as foreign exchange and money market operations, although the systems for these two classes of trading differ in certain respects. This is due to the different networks which support securities trading on the one hand and currency and money trading on the other, and the different market practices and settlement systems in these markets.

The problem

Consider the confirmation and settlement processes for securities transactions in a typical fund management operation. At virtually every step manual intervention is required: the entry of the deal slips, recording details of unconfirmed deals and programme trades, entry of broker deal confirmations, visual matching of broker deal confirmations received by telex, fax or as contract notes through the post with system listings of deal slips, the annotation of the listings with the matching broker confirmation references. Then the settlement details of the trades have to be entered into the system, which attempts to match them with unconfirmed deal records. Where this fails there is the further manual process of resolution of deal errors and the re-entry of corrected order details. So far, we have just described deal entry. Deals may have to be cancelled or amended, with further manual intervention and there may be further re-keying in order to transmit instructions to custodians if automated links are not in place, as well as manual reconciliation with the custodian. And all this against the background of settlement cycles in equity markets generally being reduced to match those of bond markets. With only three days in which to settle in CREST in the London market for instance, it is vital to be in a position to resolve problems quickly, based on accurate information. Nor is this pressure on the fund managers alone. The brokers, custodians and market makers are similarly affected. Depositories such as CREST are exerting the pressure, acting as agents of an efficient, liquid market.

The process is similar for FOREX and money market transactions but trading practices are somewhat different. Many trades are confirmed orally with written confirmation to follow. Consider the following statistics for one major institutional fund manager. Half the FOREX and money market transactions are confirmed verbally on the day of trading with postal confirmation received the following day. Of the rest, only 10 per cent are confirmed the same day by fax, while the remaining 40 per cent are confirmed by post only. Given the short time scales for treasury settlement, this means that settlement instructions for some 40 per cent of transactions are issued without first confirming the deal details with the market. This experience, which is strictly contrary to best market practice, is being repeated all over the market.

Implementing straight-through processing

How do you put straight-through processing together? The best answer to this question is in stages, rather than all at once. Although the actual sequence is a matter for the individual institution, the first step is likely to be the implementation of ETC. There are two reasons for this. First, most institutions carry out a much higher volume of securities trading, particularly equities, than money and therefore the benefit from reduced error rates in this area will be commensurately higher. Second, the installation of an ETC package and service has relatively little direct impact on a firm's other trading and back office systems. Figure 7.1 presents a simplified, logical view of the components of an ETC system.

The fund manager requires three or four system components: an ETC terminal (which may be a physical terminal or a piece of software) to communicate with the ETC service; a messenger system, which is a software component which receives messages from a counterparty in SWIFT, ETC or telex format, translates it into a form which the trade matching system can understand and forwards the message to the third component, the trade matching system. This package will carry out the actual matching of

Figure 7.1 The key elements of electronic trade confirmation for securities

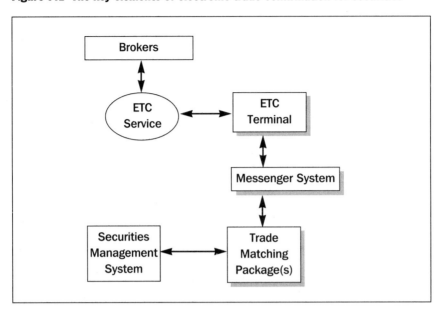

allegations with trades, or generate exception processing actions in the case of mis-matches. It will communicate accordingly with the firm's existing securities management system. Where matching is effective it will initiate the transmission of an affirmation message, which the messenger system will translate into the appropriate format for transmission by the ETC terminal over the ETC service to the counterparty, typically the broker. So the circle is completed.

Turning to the money side, the picture is similar. The key interface is to SWIFT and hence the institution needs a SWIFT terminal or SWIFT Interface Device (SID), because the standard network in the FOREX and money markets, where many of the players are banks, is SWIFT. Similarly the message format standards are all set by SWIFT. The Messenger system is common and the trade matching package carries out exactly analogous functions in respect of FX and money market trades, interfacing to the firm's treasury system. Put these two together and you have a full ETC system, Figure 7.2.

Figure 7.2 The key elements of electronic trade confirmation

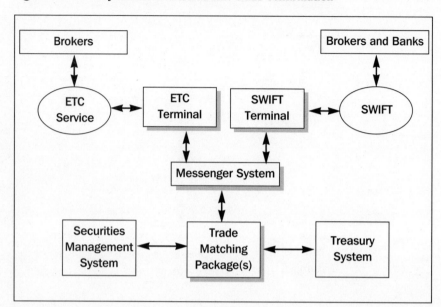

Now that ETC vendors are allowed to use SWIFT, it may in time be unnecessary to interface to two ETC networks. However, it is unlikely that all an institution's counterparties will use SWIFT. Therefore for the time being, it is likely that both services will be required. Of course many custodians are still linked to their fund management customers by proprietary links which they have developed, partly to provide a more efficient service and partly to lock those customers in. However the trend in this field (as in so many others) is towards open, that is non-proprietary networks. In ETC that effectively means SWIFT.

Once these links and systems are in place, the fund manager can enter its trade at its terminal and effect trade confirmation and matching of the bargain, whether for securities, FX or money, without manual intervention.

The next step is to move to electronic trade settlement (ETS). This enables settlement instructions to be received and matched with a pre-defined or previous instruction set, payment instruc-

Figure 7.3 The key elements of electronic trade settlement

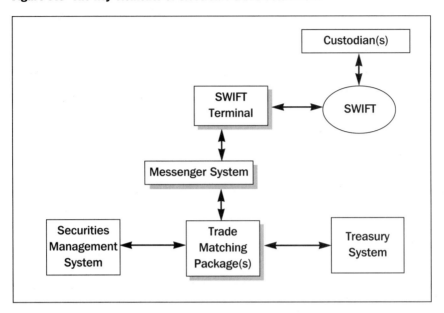

tions to be authorized and sent to custodians and settlement con-firmation details to be received from them. As Figure 7.3 shows, the architecture of the system is essentially the same as for ETC. The function of the messenger system is similar, providing a translation and a routing facility between the various networks the firm uses and the trade settlement package or packages, typically but not necessarily in SWIFT message formats. The settlement packages themselves provide the settlement facilities to interface to the firm's securities management and treasury systems.

The final step is automated reconciliation of holdings of securities and cash between the institution's systems and the cus-todian's. This is a well-established practice in the banking market, where automated nostro reconciliation is provided by a wide variety of packages, but it is still in its infancy in securities, where, of course, the problems to be solved are more challenging. Put all these components together in an integrated system and you have straight-through processing, illustrated in Figure 7.5.

Figure 7.4 The key elements of automated reconciliation

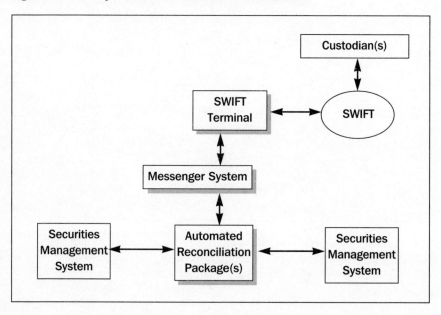

Figure 7.5 Integration gives straight-through processing

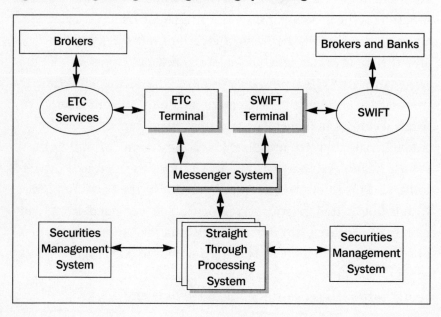

Guidelines for success

Like any significant information technology project, successful implementation of straight-through processing depends on rigorous adherence to the best practice IT disciplines which the financial services sector so often ignores to its cost. It is essential to produce a precise business requirements specification as part of an invitation to tender for potential vendors to respond to. Packages procured may be enhanced but should not be changed. Interfaces between software components require detailed specification and tight control. Packages, interfaces and bespoke software all require exhaustive testing, including regression testing when anything previously tested changes.

Beyond these disciplines, there are additional factors which can affect the ease of implementation and its success. We have already discussed the staging and sequence of component installation. We have referred to packages, implying that there is no need to write this software in-house. Indeed that is the case, since there is a thriving package software industry serving this need. Further, it is these vendors who have the greatest interest in keeping their systems up to date with the changing standards in the industry, the advent of new networks, the implementation of new clearing and settlement systems as each market strives to shorten its settlement cycle.

There is one other important issue to consider. Should you obtain the various components discussed here from one supplier, perhaps a network vendor, or go for 'best of breed' components from a variety of suppliers? The answer may depend on the availability of interfaces to your chosen network, securities management system or treasury system. If a vendor offers a standard interface to the network or system of your choice, and can demonstrate that interface being used in production, that is far more attractive than an offer to build the interface or a claim that it is not difficult to produce. However in this context, the probability of success must be enhanced if all the components can be obtained from one source, since this minimizes the number of software interfaces that have to be maintained and places the responsibility for implementation and support in one place. This may not be available, but it is worth looking for. It means that you need to define the complete path to straight-through processing before starting down it.

What are the benefits?

The prize at the end of all this effort is real. In terms of risk, the benefits are better risk control through acting on timely information, enhanced auditability, and compliance with industry best practice and regulatory requirements. Cost can be reduced by meeting settlement deadlines on a consistent basis; the ability to use new custodians and trade with new counterparties without consequent changes to systems; and the ability to handle market surges or growth in volume without adding staff in the back office. The flexibility of the business is increased by being able to accommodate changes in industry practice, new technology and new network offerings without fundamental system change. Finally the elimination or drastic reduction of manual reconciliation offers reduction not only of errors and therefore cost but also of boredom. What a prize!

GLOBAL CUSTODY TECHNOLOGY HARDWARE

I must confess to finding computer hardware much less interesting than computer systems or software. However, a chapter on global custody technology would be incomplete without some discussion of hardware used in global custody.

There are four major types of global custody technology hardware. Most systems will use at least two of these four elements:

- the mainframe computer
- the minicomputer
- the personal computer (PC)
- the communications link.

The mainframe computer, minicomputer and PC nowadays differ more in terms of the functions to which they are applied than in terms of their speed and power of data processing, storage and memory retrieval. The old hierarchy of the mainframe computer being the most powerful computer, the minicomputer the second most powerful and the PC the least powerful still gives a general impression of the difference between these three types of device, but great strides in the technology of the central processor have considerably blurred the differences.

Today, many minicomputers – such as the IBM ASI4OO, the Sun workstation, or the HP9000 – are carrying out tasks which even as little as five years ago would usually have been carried out by mainframes. Now that extremely powerful minicomputers are widely available in the financial community, mainframes are rarely required except in applications where on-line transaction processing (OLTP) – that is, real-time processing of what are usually large volumes of transactions – is carried out, for example, a nationwide automated teller machine (ATM) or debit card network. However, OLTP applications are rarely carried out by a global custodian's clients (which is not to say they will not be carried out by other divisions of the client's organization). In practice, investors will rarely need a machine more powerful than a minicomputer or PC to carry out any in-house application. Note that the power of many PCs – notably the Sun Workstation and similar machines – rivals that of many minicomputers.

The communications system refers to the link between the investor and the custodian which allows data communications to pass from one to the other. As we saw above, the communications themselves will usually pass across leased or proprietary telephone lines.

The most common piece of hardware which investors install in their offices to communicate electronically with their custodians is a stand-alone PC (i.e. a PC not networked to any other PC in the office), linked to the custodian via a data communications system. The PC will often be supplied by the custodian to the investor as part of the custody service.

The PC enables the communications process to be interactive, and facilitates the relaying of important information to the in-house system, usually through the use of floppy discs. Alternatively, the PC could be networked; either within the office in a local area network (LAN), or to other offices in a wide area network (WAN). The advantage of the networked configuration is that all the custody-related information will be available to all authorized persons having access to a PC on the network.

Another approach is to port (i.e. connect) the communications link into the investor's in-house integrated investment management administration system. These systems are widely used within the investment management community and facilitate the handling of a portfolio and the consequent management issues. These systems do not usually make specific recommendations regarding the purchase of investments; for this the investor would tend to use a front office decision support system. Investment management administration systems are back office systems. Popular examples of such systems are ACT's Quasar system, the Datastream Icon system, and DST International's HiPortfolio and Paladign systems. Alternatively, many large investors will have developed their own proprietary systems.

There are considerable advantages in porting a global custody communications link to an investment management administration system. The incoming information can be rapidly reprocessed and configured, and made available to all staff using the system. Valuation information coming in from the custodian is particularly important in this respect, but all custodian-originated information is useful.

TECHNOLOGY COMPATABILITY

The communications link between the investor and custodian will only work properly, if at all, if the communications systems used by the investor and the custodian are compatible. Generally, however, this is no longer the problem it once was. The continually increasing internationalization of the global custody industry has led to the creation of two standards which are themselves almost identical and, which is more to the point, are fully compatible.

These standards are the SWIFT standard (SWIFT is discussed in detail above), the FIX standard and the Industry Standard for Institutional Trade Communications (ISITC). An investor must ensure that whichever custodian or custodians it finally chooses, its own data communications systems are compatible with those used by the custodian or custodians.

THE COST OF GLOBAL CUSTODY TECHNOLOGY

There is no reason for an investor to spend a vast amount of money on global custody technology. If a stand-alone PC is used, this should ideally have a Pentium processor and maximum storage and memory capacity. However, the cost of such a PC, and the modem that is needed to link it into the global custodian's system, will be relatively modest.

The cost of linking the global custody system to a packaged investment management administration system or to a customized system will vary according to whether new software needs to be designed or purchased in order to complete the job. Most packages can be readily adapted to take in a feed from the custodian; some will already have the port in place. For investors contemplating purchasing an investment management administration system, the easy availability, or otherwise, of a port which can be used by the global custodian ought to be an important factor in the purchase decision process.

Some custodians prefer to use their own proprietary communications system rather than SWIFT or ISITC, although the proprietary system may still be compatible with these standards. Sometimes the global custodian will offer the investor a PC to link into its proprietary system, with the PC being offered at low cost or free of charge. Such an arrangement is often highly favourable to the investor. However, some custodians seem to think their clients ought to pay handsomely for the privilege of using the custodian's proprietary system, and this attitude ought not to be encouraged. Generally, with custody technology as with other types of financial technology, there is a distinct trend away from proprietary systems of all kinds in favour of systems and protocols that are open to anybody who uses technology featuring that protocol (such systems that are open in this way are known, simply, as 'open' systems).

It is essential that when selecting the custodian the investor looks into the technological implications of choosing a particular custodian.

THE SECURITY OF GLOBAL CUSTODY TECHNOLOGY

I have already emphasized the importance of security in the context of electronic data communications and the use of the Internet. It is now necessary to emphasize, generally, the importance of the investor's global custody technology resources – like all its technology – being protected effectively against the following hazards:

- illicit access to data by an unauthorized person;
- deliberate interference with data;
- disruption to availability;
- accidental damage.

The investor therefore needs to have a workable computer security procedure in place. Computer security can be defined as 'protecting the confidentiality, integrity and availability of a computer system and its information'.

A computer security breach is any actual breach in the confidentiality, integrity and availability of the system or its information. A computer security hazard is any threat likely to cause such a breach. A preventive measure is any step taken to prevent a hazard from being realized.

As might be expected, most computer security activity is aimed at preventing breaches. However, because preventive measures can rarely be 100% successful, a security strategy must also include measures to detect the occurrence of a breach, and corrective measures which will as far as practicable remedy the effects of a breach.

Most investors will need expert advice on maximizing the security of their global custody technology. Their custodian can often provide this advice, or recommend an expert to provide it. The information which the custodian sends should be protected against illicit access by encryption (encoding) – which makes it impossible for an unauthorized person to read it – as well as by message authentication, which alerts the recipient to any illicit interference with the message in transit.

The investor should also be careful to restrict access to its own PCs and other computer terminals to authorized persons. The best way of achieving this is to restrict physical access to the rooms where the terminals are located, and to enforce the use of a password or personal access code to restrict operation of the terminal to authorized persons. The terminal access control system should ideally create an audit trail – a detailed record of which password or code number was used to access a particular terminal at what time, and for how long. This way, if any illicit activity takes place or is suspected, the investor will have a comprehensive record of usage of a terminal.

Finally, an essential precaution against accidental damage to hardware or software – including accidental erasure or corruption of storage media – is to ensure that all data held on file in the office is fully backed up on at least *two* constantly updated additional storage media which can be brought into action immediately.

However, if the investor is a major institutional investor or an investment management organization with numerous clients of its own, merely backing up storage media is unlikely to be sufficient protection. A replacement hardware facility, with computers and communications equipment ready to operate on the investor's behalf at no more than a few hours' notice, will probably also be required. It is possible to reduce the cost of such alternative facilities (often referred to as disaster recovery facilities) by subscribing to a facility shared with other financial institutions. The chances of more than one institution needing to use the facility, simultaneously, are remote (although a plan should be in place to cover this contingency), and a facility to which several institutions subscribe will be much cheaper. Even so, many large investment management organizations prefer to have their own facility.

The investment management organization must also install in-house protection against loss of external electrical power. This usually consists of a series of dry or wet batteries to provide automatic back-up for up to about an hour against sudden power loss, and a generator facility to provide electrical power thereafter.

Investors that are not institutional investors or investment management organizations (and that therefore do not have clients of their own) must decide how critical to their operation accidental damage to or loss of power to their computer resources would be, and make contingency plans accordingly.

THE CHALLENGE OF LEGACY SYSTEMS

The reader will hardly be unaware that one challenge currently facing most computer systems is the so-called 'Millennium problem', a term used to describe the serious problem that many computer systems currently used within industry and commerce – including those used in the investments and securities industries – do not feature full Year 2000 compatibility, that is, they are unable to handle dates after and including 1 January 2000 without the system regarding the '00' at the end of the 2000 as indicative that the year is really 1900. The reason for this is that many computer systems were written by programmers who thought it would be fine to include only a two-digit programming field for the year. This was fine when the Year 2000 was 20 or 30 years way, but it is hardly fine now. A similar problem is that many financial systems are not compatible with the Euro which obviously has particular implications for institutional investors operating cross-border investment portfolios. I say more about global custody and the Euro in Chapter 8.

Generally, technology used by investors and their custodians has to be especially adept at dealing with multi-currency positions and must certainly feature Year 2000 and Euro compatibility.

Most large institutional investors are already working hard to ensure that their systems have the correct compatibility for the new millennium and for the Euro. Global custodians are also working with urgency to achieve these compatabilities if they have not achieved them already. There is not much else to say here about this problem other than that something must be done about it right away.

CONCLUSION

In this chapter I looked at the enormously important role of technology in helping investors get the most from global custody. I emphasized the importance of the use of technology in the custody process and made clear that it is far from being the case that all custodians are sufficiently automated. I set down precisely why technology is so important to investors who use custody services and also emphasized its importance as a means of communication.

I then turned to considering the Internet and its role in custody and looked at some of the key security issues related to the Internet.

Finally, I considered certain international message-switching services and looked at straight through-processing and how an investor can typically provide itself with this facility. I concluded by considering the basic nature of global custody technology and considered some of the major challenges facing investors, especially in relation to updating their systems to become 'Millennium compliant'.

THE FUTURE — 8

INTRODUCTION

The past five years have been a time of enormous change for the global custody industry. Many formerly apparently successful players have left it, others have merged with former rivals to create a new, giant bank which may incorporate the names of its constituents, or else cause one to disappear. Intense competition over fees has brought them right down, although they are now starting to show signs of rising again. New technology, and especially the Internet and the increasing interest in straight-through processing, have brought into the foreground exciting new possibilities for utilizing, respectively, this highly innovative communications system and potentially fault-free processing mechanism.

There is also a discernible trend whereby big custodians are getting bigger, often by takeover or merger, in order to create an entity with the enormous resources required to compete with other enormous players. Generally, medium-sized global custodians are finding it difficult to tread water, let alone reach the golden sands of a sun-drenched shore. On the other hand, smaller domestic custodians with real expertise in a local market seem to be having no real problems holding their own In the future we are likely to see a few very large global custodians and many small domestic custodians.

So great is the flux within the global custody industry that in five years' time it will most likely also be possible to say that 'the past five years have been a time of enormous change' for the industry. Indeed, the fact that the global custody industry, so interesting and exciting, is in a constant state of dynamic change seems part of its very being. The state of rapid change results in part from the constant demands investors place on custodians for ever-improved levels of service, and partly from the sheer energy of the competitiveness between custodians to excel and deliver first-rate services. In fact, in an article I wrote in 1995 about the global custody industry I concluded, 'The global custody industry of the future will be even more dynamic than the already intense and ultra-competitive industry of today.' This has proved true, and will probably also prove true in the future.

There is one factor for change which is very much a feature of the last years of the Millennium. This factor is the Euro, which is now upon us. It affects everyone with the remotest involvement in global custody in Europe.

The reasons for the Euro coming into existence in the first place, and the pros and cons of the system, are not my province here. Neither is the debate over whether certain individual countries which have elected to become part of this new currency from 1 January 1999 should have done so, or whether countries which did not join from the inauguration date should in fact have joined. My only interest in the Euro as far as this book is concerned is its implications for global custody.

With the inauguration date for the Euro now behind us, much of the work that was necessary to get the new currency up and running has already been completed. As things turned out, there was not the securities reconciliation nightmare that everybody was expecting. The problem of re-denomination was a formidable one, but there is a general consensus that the global custody and securities industry dealt with the strain effectively.

There are obviously new lessons that everybody has to learn.

New skills are being developed so that custodians can become adept at securities reconciliation and cash reconciliation in the Euro dispensation. New skills are also being developed in the management of odd lots of securities, which in the traditional national currencies had a value which was a round number but which is no longer a round number of Euros. Portfolio balancing is also being undertaken with energy and decisiveness.

Generally, the introduction of the Euro has not caused any major problems for the global custody industry. In the future, one may confidently expect the new currency to make a major contribution to streamlining the efficiency of the securities industry, and by extension that of the global custody business.

Obviously the medium-term hope is that 11 local Euro markets will become, in effect, one regional market. It is clearly too early to know whether this will, in fact, happen. Incidentally, I should say that I have written this last chapter of the book a month or so later than the rest of the material in order to accommodate the events of 1 January 1999. The book is going to press at a time when the precise impact of the Euro on global custody in Europe is uncertain. In future editions of this book I hope to have the chance to enlarge on the matter.

Another, if less topical, major trend governing the future of the global custody industry is the continuing, increasing institutionalization of domestic and global investment assets. What this means is that an ever-increasing proportion of domestic and global investment assets are being handled by institutional investors. This development is proceeding hand-in-hand with a continuing escalation in the rise in the proportion of cross-border investments as a proportion of all investments.

The increasing institutionalization of investments stems from the sheer arithmetic of the billions of dollars of premiums and contributions that are being invested every working day in institutional investors' organizations. The escalation in cross-border investments is a consequence of the simple fact that, leaving aside occasional blips of nationalistic fervour, the world is becoming more of a global village.

Increasing speed and efficiency of communications technology, decreases in real terms in the cost of international air travel, and a global cultural climate where, on the whole, the battle between capitalism and communism has been replaced by the battle to make money and to own consumer goods (undoubtedly a healthier battle, for all its cultural hazards), all play a role in the globalization of the world. The principal factor in the rise in cross-border investment is, however, more straightforward: institutional and private investors are increasingly coming to believe that the risk/return profile offered by foreign investment is something they cannot do without.

FUTURE REQUIREMENTS FOR SUCCESSFUL GLOBAL CUSTODIANS

In the future, global custodians that seek not only to survive but also to thrive must wholeheartedly pursue a total commitment to the industry, as well as an absolute commitment to breadth, reliability and quality of customer service. They must also be able to demonstrate significant capitalization (probably a minimum of $500 million), and must be willing to spend heavily on new operational and technological infrastructures without needing to see an instant return on the capital.

They also need an ability to recruit the very best staff, keep them, and provide a rewarding and intellectual environment where the staff carry out their very best work for clients. The custodians must also have a willingness to play a leading public role as a major industry participant in terms of influencing legislation and speaking out on leading industry issues. That custodians also need a determination not only to excel, but to be the best, almost goes without saying.

THE TREND FOR LARGE CORPORATES TO OUTSOURCE GLOBAL CUSTODY SERVICES

Another important trend in global custody is the increasing readiness of large corporate investors to outsource custody services rather than attempt to undertake custody themselves, this is going to continue. The trend is already well-marked in the UK and US, and in future we may expect to see it developing in Continental Europe and other areas where there is not, at present, a culture where investors outsource global custody services.

THE TREND TOWARDS CONSOLIDATION

I think we will also see an increasing tendency towards consolidation of global custody services, with large corporates preferring to source their custody from one major global custodian rather than from a variety of custodians in a network which the investor may in some cases attempt to manage itself.

DEVELOPMENTS IN SECURITIES LENDING AND REPOS

On a more technical note, I am confident that we will see a rapid escalation in the use of securities lending and repos as methods of covering positions in cost-effective ways.

We have already discussed securities lending in detail. The other technique, the repo, is somewhat different. A repo, which is simply an abbreviation for 'repurchase agreement' is an agreement which involves a commitment by the seller to buy a security – usually a bond – back from the purchaser at a specified price at a designated future date. Basically it represents a collateralized short-term loan, with the collateral typically being a bond, money market instrument, Federal agency security or mortgage-backed security. A repo has the advantage that it can be used to fund a trader's or investor's book, as the trader or investor can buy a security under a repo agreement, use the security as it thinks fit, and then known that the security will have a definite cash value in the future. Both traders and investors are paying more and more attention to the advantages of repos, and custodians need to understand not only how to handle these instruments but also how their fundamental dynamics work.

THE CHANGING NATURE OF THE GLOBAL CUSTODY SERVICE

The nature of the global custody service is changing fast. I have already expressed my opinion that the notion of the global custody service becoming commoditized is not enormously convincing. In fact, far from the service becoming commoditized, I detect an increase in the importance of personal service. As one London-based custodian told me;

> *'We are moving from a situation where global custody is mainly about processing transactions to one where the transaction processing capability is taken for granted and where what really matters is the quality of the information that the custodian is providing.'*

This information is being provided in electronic format and

across an ever-increasing number of markets. It is perfectly possible that by the new century only a relatively small number of markets will still be 'emerging markets' in the sense that their infrastructures and procedures are antiquated, largely paper-based, full of risk and generally not very secure. Developing nations are becoming thoroughly aware that if they want to attract foreign indirect (or direct) investment they need to get their infrastructures for the financial markets into gear. This development is, of course, a very welcome one. The better the condition of national securities market infrastructures, the better for everyone.

There is also likely to be an increasing trend towards the awareness of the risks that custodians bear and an increasing insistence, on the part of the investor, that custodians should minimize their own risks, whether this minimization stems from increasing the efficiency and the effectiveness with which custody services are carried out, or from protecting custodians' operations against fraud, incompetence, and accidental or deliberate loss of all kinds. We have already seen how recent UK legislation in effect urges investors to be extremely demanding of custodians. The custodian is expected to demonstrate that it has already minimized its risks throughout its organization. Legislation also urges investors to demand that custodians that have not yet completed a comprehensive risk audit do so.

As for technology itself, the importance of this within the global custody industry is almost certain to increase in the future. I imagine that within five years or so, most, if not all custodians of all kinds around the world will be almost entirely automated in how they deal with the need to process transactions and how they handle all other services which are capable of being automated.

But I would close by again emphasizing the importance of personal service: an importance which, logically, is only likely to grow as automation of routine processes becomes even more widespread than it is today. Ultimately, custodians can only offer a first-rate service when they truly understand and empathize with what their investor clients are seeking to do. There is thus no substitute for the dynamic desire on the part of a custodian to meet its investor clients' needs, and ideally anticipate them.

As so often in business, a service which starts out by looking impossibly technical and obscure, turns out, after all, to be based closely around a positive and fruitful relationship between customer and supplier.

INDEX